FULL of FLAVOR

MARIA ELIA

Maria Elia was brought up at the stove of her Greek Cypriot father's restaurant. Her love of cooking has grown into a passion that has led her to travel the world and incorporate an eclectic range of influences into her cooking style—earning her great acclaim when head chef at Delfina's and the Whitechapel Gallery Dining Room in London. Maria is currently Executive Chef for Joe's in London, England. She is also a contributor to *Olive* and *Good Food* magazine and appears regularly on TV.

www.thisismariaelia.com

FULL
of
FLAVOR

How to create like a chef

MARIA ELIA

Photography by Jonathan Gregson

K

Kyle Books

Published in 2013 by Kyle Books
an imprint of Kyle Cathie Limited
www.kylebooks.com

Distributed by National Book Network
4501 Forbes Blvd., Suite 200
Lanham, MD 20706
Phone: (800) 462-6420
Fax: (301) 429-5746
custserv@nbnbooks.com

First published in Great Britain in 2011 by
Kyle Books Limited

10 9 8 7 6 5 4 3 2 1

978-1-906868-58-1

Photographer: Jonathan Gregson
Designer and Illustrator: Kath Harding
Project Editor: Jenny Wheatley
Home Economist: Annie Rigg
Prop Stylist: Liz Belton
Copy Editor: Anne Newman
Proofreader: Nikki Sims
Editorial Assistant: Estella Hung
Production: Nic Jones and David Hearn

Library of Congress Control Number: 2012945601

Color reproduction by XY Digital Ltd in the UK
Printed in China by C&C Offset Printing Co. Ltd

DEDICATION
To my Mom and Dad,
for showing me the
path to succeed.

COOK'S NOTES

Butter is unsalted unless otherwise stated

Always make sure fish is from a sustainable source

Eggs should always be free-range and are medium
unless otherwise specified

Milk should be organic and 1% unless otherwise stated

CONTENTS

CREATING WITH FLAVOR

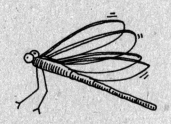

HOW do I combine flavors? Well, over the years I've built up a memory bank of tastes. I combine flavors in my mind and envision how they will taste on a plate. I'll usually sketch the dish and color it in; thinking about flavor, texture, and presentation. Everything is carefully thought about, and cooking in my head and then sketching it helps me to understand a dish before it becomes a reality.

I also like to draw "mind maps." I'll think of an ingredient and take it on a mental adventure, noting every possible complementary flavor. Each chapter in this book opens with a simplified version of one of my mind maps, to give insight into how I've come up with some of the recipes in that chapter.

The recipes in this book are inspired by my culinary experiences and my extensive travels through work and pleasure. Some have been created through experimentation, and some by improvisation.

I want the dishes in this book to help your palate come alive and in turn you can make the recipes your own by taking them on a flavor journey. I've included a "Take It Further" section at the end of the book, complete with notepaper, for you to take pen to paper and document your own variations.

The challenge in writing this book was transferring what goes on in my head onto a piece of paper! So what I decided to do was to break down my thought process. There are several areas that I focus on when creating a new dish, as follows.

THE MAIN INGREDIENT

FOR me, the main ingredient is the starting point when creating a new recipe. That's why I've arranged the book around 18 of my favorite ingredients, including lamb, eggplant, and chocolate.

It's important to understand the essence of an ingredient: its flavor, aroma, texture, and even appearance. The main ingredient needs respect and should be shown off to its greatest potential.

Consider the ingredient in its raw and simple state. For example, how amazing do freshly picked vine ripened tomatoes taste? All they need is a pinch of salt. From there you can add things like olive oil, basil or some feta, a touch of chile, or some anchovies. You are introducing different flavors that complement that beautiful fragrant tomato. None of the ingredients so far is spoiling the tomato in any way, they are simply taking it on a journey.

The ingredients need to be in season to give the best flavor. How great to shop at a farmers' market as opposed to a supermarket, seeing an abundance of the freshest finest ingredients, talking to the producer, and finding out about the provenance.

Working with less familiar ingredients also gets the creative juices flowing—in this book you'll find recipes starring those such as quinoa and pomelo, as well as some underused cuts of meat that won't cost the earth, such as lamb loin and beef brisket.

7

COMPLEMENTARY FLAVORS

OUR palates can detect four basic flavors: bitter, sweet, sour, and salty, and a fifth called umami. This is a Japanese word meaning flavor or taste and is described as a savory or meaty taste. It can be tasted in fermented or cured foods, Parmesan, wild mushrooms, and olives, for example. In a nutshell, it's a flavor that our palates can't get enough of!

To create with flavor is about understanding the properties of ingredients so you can combine and create a dish that satisfies the palate. Easier said than done, right? Well, the best thing about cooking is that it's a neverending learning experience, that's why I love it; the more you experiment the more you begin to understand what your palate prefers.

Let's take, for example, Slow-roasted Paprika Chicken with Butternut Squash, Smashed Butter Beans, and Tomatoes (recipe #6). The sweetness is within the squash, which soaks up the meltingly rich fatty chicken juices. The paprika provides depth of flavor with its smoky earthiness, adding a touch of heat at the same time—complementing the sweet squash. The tomatoes add acidity to liven the dish and bring it all together and the white beans provide a neutral but solid foundation. Lastly, the basil contributes aroma and freshness to perk it all up, and offers the added bonus of vibrant color.

Hopefully you are beginning to see how flavors are combined; it's about understanding a foundation recipe that works and building upon it. At the same time, it's important not to create confusion. Sometimes less is more, so don't go overboard and add so many elements that you destroy the central flavor. Add ingredients as background notes and let the main ingredient sing its song loud and clear!

USING DIFFERENT COOKING METHODS TO VARY TEXTURE

WHEN I was at the Whitechapel Gallery Dining Room I wanted to create a dish that told a story. So I created "textures of vegetables" as a main course that evolved through the seasons. For example, it may have been a "textures of cauliflower" dish. The aim was to create a plate that showed how one ingredient (and to me, vegetables seemed the most interesting) could be used in different guises. The characteristics of an ingredient can change dramatically through different cooking techniques.

For cauliflower, I served it raw as a "couscous" (see recipe #38), adding preserved lemons, mint, and pistachio to introduce texture, acidity, and a freshness to complement its unique raw flavor. Then I made a soup to which I added lemongrass, a flavor combination I'd been toying with in my mind, and a little ginger and cilantro root brought them together. The garnish was a little roasted cauliflower; again, the method of cooking gave the cauliflower a completely new flavor. A little savory panna cotta served cold added interest to the plate with a change of temperature and creaminess. Wafer-thin florets gently fried in olive oil tasted like oyster mushrooms, again a different cooking method to create another flavor.

So, on one plate several textures and flavors of a single ingredient came together in harmony. All I did was add elements to bring out the best of cauliflower.

9

way to roast a bird. Chicken is pretty neutral and combines well with most herbs and spices. So, how about making a summery marinade using chopped dill with some crushed garlic, olive oil, lemon zest, and juice, and then marinate as in the recipe. Replace the squash with some lovely baby potatoes, cut in half, toss in oil and season, place the chicken on top, and slow roast. To finish, replace the tomatoes with a squeeze of lemon juice (acidic like the tomatoes) and add some fresh blanched peas and fava beans. Lightly crush the potatoes with the peas and beans to soak up the cooking juices and again freshen it up with herbs such as flat-leaf parsley and mint. Gorgeous!

Or, take the chicken on an Asian flavor journey. Take the predominant flavors of Asian cuisine— chile, garlic, ginger, and cilantro root; crush together, mix with oil, and rub over the chicken. Use sweet potato and chopped ginger to replace the squash or even chunks of eggplant. Place the chicken on top and slow roast as normal. Finish by adding lots of chopped cilantro, a dash of soy sauce, a squeeze of lime, a splash of fish sauce, and some chopped scallions and chile.

That's what I'd love you to do with this book— cook the recipes with confidence and then begin to experiment when ingredients are out of season, say, or you need to improvise. Write the changes in the blank "Take it Further" pages at the end of the book if you loved them and begin to make this cookbook truly yours.

Where space permits I've offered variations for recipes, giving you ideas on how to vary and adapt them to suit your mood or the season. Where a recipe is more complicated, I've offered an alternative, simpler version—perhaps you may only want to take part of a recipe and not even cook the rest. That's exactly how I want you to use this book: it's not at all dictatorial, it's for you to pick and choose how you want to cook from it.

TAKING THE RECIPES FURTHER

I'D LIKE this book is to give you the confidence to develop a recipe and take it further—on your own adventure. Let's go back to the paprika chicken example (recipe #6).

Once you've tried this recipe and you're happy with it, you might wonder how you could adapt it for another time of the year when squash is not in season. If it was summer, for example, you'd want something fresher tasting. You've already learned how to spatchcock a chicken and have seen that slow roasting on the bone is a sensational

FINISHING TOUCHES

CONSIDER whether the dish needs a garnish and, if so, will it serve a purpose?

I believe garnishes should enhance a dish rather than inhibit. For instance, pea shoots used in some of my recipes are an extension of an ingredient being used—yes, peas! Or popcorn with cream of corn (see recipe #39)—it's a garnish but also within the corn family, creating a different texture.

GO FORTH AND CREATE WITH FLAVOR

I hope the recipes I've provided here give you enough confidence to experiment and go off on a "culinary adventure." To me, a recipe is more than just a set of ingredients, it's a fount of information on how to cook various ingredients that in turn guides you toward creating your own exciting dishes and flavor combinations.

I hope you find the recipes and the concept interesting. I will show you how to take them further, but predominantly I wanted this book to be about the reader. I'd like you to take this book, digest it, and make it your very own workbook. Pass your recipe variations onto your friends and family and see how they've recreated certain recipes too. That's half the fun of cooking— nurturing, sourcing, and tasting ingredients, then creating and entertaining.

So, pour yourself a glass of wine, choose some music to cook to, relax, enjoy, and cook—bliss!

11

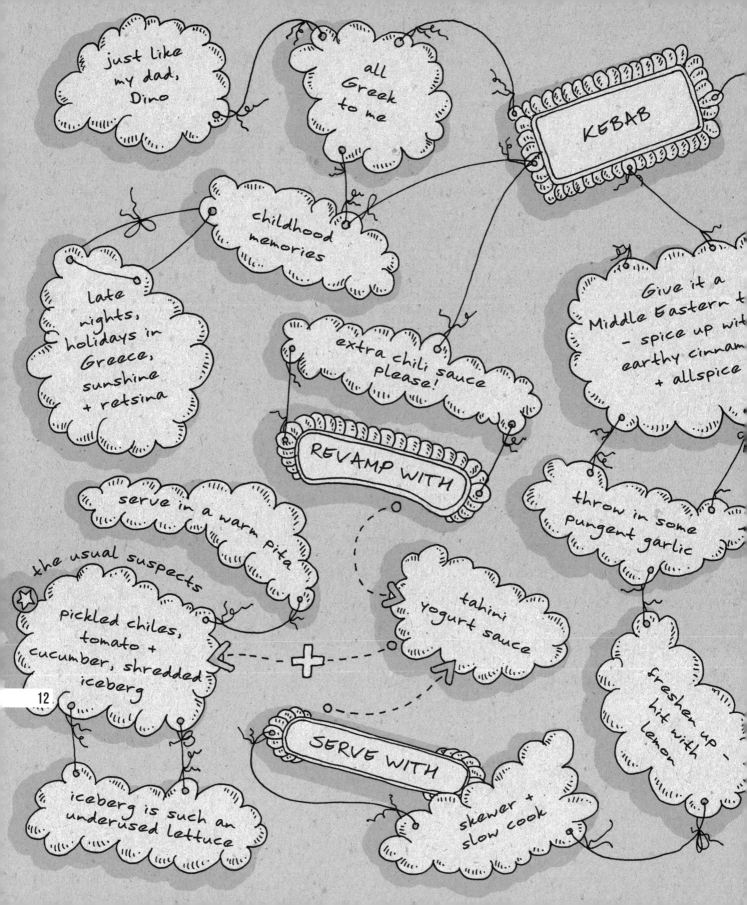

Protein-packed turkey meatballs in an Asian broth—perfect for a light lunch or post-workout meal. I taught my kick-boxing classmates this dinner! Make the meatballs the day before and reheat them in the broth. **< SERVES 4 >**

ASIAN BROTH WITH TURKEY MEATBALLS

1 quart chicken stock

1 red chile, finely sliced

1¼in piece of fresh ginger, julienned

2 lime leaves

2 tsp palm sugar

1 bok choy, separated into leaves or baby corn sliced into ½in pieces

dash of soy sauce

dash of fish sauce

FOR THE MEATBALLS

2 shallots, finely chopped

2 lime leaves, finely chopped

¾in piece of fresh ginger, grated

1 garlic clove, finely chopped

1 chile, finely chopped

1 small bunch cilantro, finely chopped

7oz ground turkey

1 egg yolk

dash of fish sauce

2 tbsp olive oil

FOR THE NOODLES

2 bunches rice noodles

1 small bunch cilantro, coarsely chopped

½ small bunch mint, chopped

12 Thai basil leaves (optional)

handful of bean sprouts

2 scallions, thinly sliced

1 lime, cut into wedges

First make the broth. Heat the chicken stock, chile, and ginger in a pan and bring to a boil. Reduce heat to a simmer, add the lime leaves and palm sugar, and cook for 5–6 minutes. Remove from the heat and set aside to infuse while you make your meatballs.

Place the shallots, lime leaves, ginger, garlic, chile, and cilantro into a food processor and pulse until combined. (Alternatively, you can mix by hand; make sure your ingredients are very finely chopped though.) Mix with the turkey, along with the egg. Season with a dash of fish sauce (this will replace salt).

Roll the mixture into small balls. Heat the oil in a frying pan, then cook the meatballs for 4–5 minutes on either side or until golden brown and cooked through.

Meanwhile, reheat the broth gently. Once simmering, add the bok choy or baby corn and cook for a minute. Add a dash of soy sauce and fish sauce to taste.

Cook or soak the noodles according to package instructions. To serve, divide the noodles between serving bowls and arrange the herbs, bean sprouts, and scallions on top. Add the meatballs, ladle over the hot broth, and garnish with lime wedges.

14

This may seem like a mammoth recipe, but it's really up to you how many of the elements you want to include. The chicken, pancetta chips, croûtons, and dressing can all be prepared beforehand. < SERVES 4 >

#2

CHICKEN CAESAR SALAD

Preheat the oven to 400°F.

Mix the lemon zest, thyme, garlic, and olive oil together, rub over the chicken, and marinate for at least an hour or overnight. Remove from the fridge half an hour before cooking. Preheat a ridged grill pan, season the chicken, and cook for 8–10 minutes on each side. Leave to rest, then slice.

Lay the pancetta on a baking sheet, cover with parchment paper, and place another baking sheet on top. Bake for 10–15 minutes, or until browned and crisp. Remove baking sheet and paper and drizzle immediately with maple syrup, sprinkle with pepper, and leave to cool.

To make the croûtons, tear the bread into ¾in rustic chunks and spread over a large baking sheet. Drizzle with olive oil and sea salt and mix to coat the bread. Bake in the oven for about 8 minutes until golden and crisp on the outside, but chewy on the inside.

For the dressing, place the eggs, vinegar, anchovies, Parmesan, garlic, and mustard in a blender. Process to a smooth purée, add the lemon juice, and slowly pour in the oil with the motor running.

For the salad, preheat a ridged grill pan. Halve and quarter the gem lengthwise and brush with olive oil. Season with sea salt and pepper, then grill on both sides, until the leaves have taken on some color and wilted slightly. Remove from the heat. You can serve these hot or cold.

For the eggs, fill a pan with water, add the vinegar, and bring to a boil. Crack the eggs into cups. Once the water is boiling, stir to create a gentle whirlpool. Carefully slide the eggs into the water, one at a time, and adjust the heat so the water simmers gently. Cook for 3 minutes, then remove the eggs with a slotted spoon and season.

To assemble the salad, spoon a little dressing onto each plate and place the gem quarters on top. Add a couple of croûtons and the sliced chicken. Spoon over more dressing and top with a poached egg. Scatter over the Parmesan and more croûtons, garnish with the pancetta chips, and serve.

zest of 1 lemon
2 tsp thyme leaves
1 garlic clove, crushed
a good dash of olive oil
2 boneless, skinless chicken breasts
sea salt and black pepper

FOR THE PANCETTA CHIPS
8–12 thin slices pancetta
2 tbsp maple syrup

FOR THE CROÛTONS
½ ciabatta loaf
a good dash of olive oil

FOR THE DRESSING
1 egg
½ teaspoon white wine vinegar
5 salted anchovies
¼ cup Parmesan, grated (plus extra to serve)
1 garlic cloves
1 tsp Dijon mustard
juice of ½ lemon
½ cup extra virgin olive oil

FOR THE SALAD
4 baby gem lettuces
olive oil

FOR THE POACHED EGGS
4 eggs
dash of malt vinegar

17

#3

I love good old "poule au pot" and am surprised at how many people have never poached a whole chicken. It is a low-fat method of cooking that keeps the chicken succulent and flavorful. < SERVES 4 >

POACHED CHICKEN

1 whole medium-sized chicken

4 celery ribs, coarsely chopped

1 onion, coarsely chopped

2 carrots, peeled and coarsely chopped

4 whole garlic cloves

2 bay leaves

few parsley stems and sprigs of thyme

4 whole black peppercorns

1 glass (approximately ½ cup) white wine (optional— you may prefer to drink it!)

Remove any giblets from your chicken and place in a large pot with the celery, onion, carrots, garlic, herbs, peppercorns, and white wine. Add enough cold water to cover the chicken well.

Place the pot over medium-high heat and slowly bring to a simmer, making sure the liquid does not boil, or the chicken will be tough. Cook gently for 1 hour, then remove from the heat, immediately cover, and allow to stand for another hour—the chicken will continue to cook gently.

Remove the chicken from the liquid and leave to cool before serving. Strain the liquid through a sieve and discard the vegetables, herbs, and peppercorns. Skim off any fat and set aside the broth. If you're making in advance, refrigerate the whole chicken in the cooled cooking liquid.

That's the basic recipe, but you're probably wondering what to do with this whole chicken. You can create a world of flavors from this base recipe—read on for ideas.

VARIATIONS

- Use the liquid to poach vegetables and noodles in for an Asian chicken and noodle soup, finishing with fresh cilantro, scallions, Thai fish sauce, and a dash of soy sauce.
- The legs can be removed and used in a pasta dish or a risotto.
- The breast can be removed and sliced, and used for Vietnamese Rice Paper Rolls (recipe #46) or in the Chicken Caesar Salad (recipe #2).
- For an Asian twist, replace the herbs with a split chile, lime leaves, lemongrass, star anise, and ginger.
- You can also save the liquid to cook a risotto in; I like to use it to soak dried porcinis in for a double flavor hit if I'm making a chicken and porcini risotto.
- The broth can be made into a "veloute," the equivalent of a béchamel where the milk is replaced with stock and finished with cream.
- Use the chicken in a fragrant Asian salad dressed with *nam jim*.
- Poached chicken also makes the best sandwiches!

18

Hot, comforting, and full of goodness—perfect for a winter's day! It's also a great way to use the chicken and poaching liquid from the recipe opposite. < SERVES 2 (REALLY 4, BUT YOU'LL WANT TO GO BACK FOR SECONDS!)>

CHICKEN, BARLEY, AND VEGETABLE SOUP

Heat the oil in a large saucepan. Gently cook the onion, leek, garlic, carrot, and celery, stirring, until softened. Add the mushrooms and cook for another 5 minutes. Pour in the cooking liquid or stock and bring to a boil. Add the barley and simmer for 20 minutes. Add the chicken, season with salt and pepper, and cook for another 10 minutes or until the barley is tender.

Check the seasoning and stir in the herbs, spinach, and cream, if using, and serve immediately.

VARIATIONS

- If I'm not adding cream, I like to serve the soup drizzled with olive oil and topped with a little shaved Parmesan.
- If you prefer a tomato-flavored version, add some peeled and diced tomatoes in the last 10 minutes of cooking.
- Vary your herbs to create your own flavorful soup.
- Substitute the barley with another grain, such as faro, quinoa, or even amaranth—you will need to adjust the timings though, depending on the grain. Pre-soaking speeds up the cooking time.

3 tbsp olive oil

1 large onion, finely chopped

1 leek, finely chopped

2 garlic cloves, finely chopped

2 carrots, finely chopped

4 celery ribs, finely chopped

1lb 2oz chestnut mushrooms, finely sliced

1½ quarts chicken stock or cooking liquid from a whole poached chicken (see opposite)

6oz pearl barley, soaked in cold water overnight, then drained

picked meat from 2 chicken legs or breasts

sea salt and black pepper

1 small bunch tarragon, leaves stripped and finely chopped

a handful of flat-leaf parsley, finely chopped

2 handfuls of baby spinach (optional)

¾ cup cream, optional, if you want a creamy finish

Hot pita bread filled with delicious tender chicken, pickled chile peppers, and fresh crisp salad... it's not just because I'm half Greek that I love a good kebab. This one is famous at my annual summer barbecue. < SERVES 4–6 >

MIDDLE EASTERN KEBAB

FOR THE MARINADE
4 garlic cloves
2 tsp sea salt
pinch of black pepper
juice of 1 lemon
4 tbsp olive oil
1½ tbsp ground cinnamon
2 tbsp ground allspice

12 boneless, skinless
chicken thighs

TO SERVE
warm pita bread
iceberg lettuce, shredded
tomato, cucumber, and red
onions, thinly sliced
pickled chile peppers
(optional)
Tahini Yogurt Sauce
(recipe #103)

you will need two 12in
metal skewers

In a large mortar and pestle, crush the garlic cloves with the sea salt and black pepper, then stir in the lemon juice, olive oil, and spices. Place the chicken in a shallow dish, pour in the marinade, and coat well. Refrigerate for at least 1 hour or overnight.

Preheat the oven to 325°F.

Fold a chicken thigh in half and thread widthwise onto the two skewers. The skewers should be 1¼in apart to make the kebab sturdy. Repeat with remaining 11 chicken thighs to form a solid kebab.

Place the skewered chicken on a hot ridged grill pan and sear on each side. Transfer to a baking sheet and finish in the oven for 40 minutes, turning halfway through cooking. Set aside the cooking juices and pour over the chicken before serving.

To serve, hold the kebab on a cutting board, point-side down, and slice off the meat using a sharp knife.

Serve with the warm pita bread, salad, pickled chile peppers, and tahini yogurt sauce.

I simply love smoked paprika—the deep, earthy flavors of spice and heat make this dish lip-smackingly great. If you have time, marinate the chicken for at least four hours or the day before. < SERVES 4 >

#6

SLOW-ROASTED PAPRIKA CHICKEN WITH BUTTERNUT SQUASH, SMASHED BUTTER BEANS, AND TOMATOES

Preheat the oven to 350°F.

You need to spatchcock the chicken for this recipe. Calm down, it's not as scary as it sounds! First find your kitchen scissors. Remove the wing tips from the chicken. Place the chicken on a board, breast side down, and then cut along either side of the backbone to remove. Turn the chicken over and then, using the palm of your hand, press down on the chicken to make it flat. There you have it, a "spatchcock chicken"!

Place the garlic in a mortar and pestle with the salt and crush to a paste. Then add the smoked paprika and enough olive oil to make a runny paste.

Wash the butternut squash and cut into large chunks, leaving the skin on. Lay in a roasting pan, then sprinkle with sea salt and drizzle with olive oil.

Massage most of the smoked paprika paste over the breast side of the chicken, getting right into the leg joints, then rub a little on the bone side. Place on top of the squash, breast side down. Leave to marinate for an hour or refrigerate overnight. Remove from the refrigerator 30 minutes before cooking.

Place the roasting pan in the oven. After 30 minutes, turn the chicken over so the breast side is up, and baste with the juices. Lower the oven to 325°F and cook for another 1½ hours, basting every 30 minutes. Remove the chicken from the roasting pan, cover with foil, and leave to rest for 10 minutes.

Add the drained beans and tomatoes to the roasting pan and warm through while the chicken rests. Once warm, gently smash the beans with a potato masher or fork, keeping them fairly chunky. Season with sea salt and pepper, toss with the basil, and pile onto a large plate. Top with the squash. Cut the chicken in half or into quarters, depending on how hungry you and your guests are, and serve drizzled with those yummy smoky paprika chicken juices.

1 whole 3½–4½lb chicken
2 garlic cloves
sea salt and black pepper
2 tbsp smoked paprika—picante or dolce
¼ cup of olive oil
½ butternut squash, about 2¼lb
1 x 14oz can of cooked butter beans, or any other cooked white beans
7oz cherry vine tomatoes, or plum vine tomatoes
handful of Greek basil or Italian basil, coarsely chopped

23

#7

I'm not really an offal fan, but I adore this chicken liver pâté! I first tasted it on a crostini while in Castellina in Chianti many years ago, and was totally inspired. Here is my version of that dreamy dish. < **SERVES 4** >

TUSCAN CHICKEN LIVER PÂTÉ WITH FRESH FIGS

1lb 2oz chicken livers, trimmed of membranes

sea salt and black pepper

4 tbsp olive oil

1 small red onion, finely chopped

4 salted anchovies, finely chopped

¾ cup red wine

1 tbsp good-quality red wine vinegar, preferably Cabernet Sauvignon

TO SERVE

⅔ cup Cabernet Sauvignon vinegar (optional)

4 slices rosemary or plain ciabatta

drizzle of extra virgin olive oil

handful of arugula

2 fresh figs, cut into 8

Season the chicken livers with sea salt and black pepper. Heat half the olive oil in a large frying pan and gently cook the livers for 2–3 minutes. Remove the livers and set aside.

Heat the remaining olive oil in the same pan and cook the onion until soft. Add the anchovies and red wine and simmer until reduced and syrupy.

Put the livers and the onion mixture in a blender and process with the vinegar until almost smooth; season with salt and pepper and then refrigerate until required.

To make a Cabernet Sauvignon syrup, if using, pour the vinegar into a small pan and heat gently until reduced to a syrup (about 3–5 minutes). Store at room temperature.

Drizzle the ciabatta with olive oil, place on a hot ridged grill pan, and cook until crisp on both sides.

To serve, spread the pâté onto the ciabatta slices, top with arugula, and scatter with figs. Drizzle the olive oil and the Cabernet Sauvignon syrup over the top.

VARIATIONS

- Try adding some garlic and sage to your pâté and serve with fried fresh porcinis instead of figs—just as gorgeous!

24

#8 *One of my all-time favorite ways to cook duck legs! A perfect dinner party dish as you can prepare it up to three days ahead. You can buy the more unusual Asian ingredients online.* < SERVES 4 >

RED BRAISED DUCK LEGS

FOR THE BRAISING LIQUID

⅓ cup light soy sauce

⅔ cup Shaoxing or other rice wine

¾ cup yellow rock sugar

2 strips dried orange peel, or dried mandarin rind

1 red chile, pointed end slit with a sharp knife

¾in piece fresh ginger, finely sliced

1 stick cassia bark

2 star anise

4 duck legs, about 10½oz each

FOR THE SAUCE

7oz mixed mushrooms, such as shiitake, shimejis, oysters

3 tbsp sesame oil

2 garlic cloves, finely chopped

3-4 shallots, thinly sliced

¾in piece of ginger, peeled and finely chopped

1 red chile, finely sliced

1 small bunch cilantro, finely chopped

TO SERVE

cooked rice

Pickled Enoki (recipe #106)—optional

few leaves Thai basil (optional)

4 baby bok choy, blanched

Place all the braising ingredients except for the duck legs in a deep, large saucepan with 1 quart water. Bring to a boil, reduce the heat, and simmer for 15 minutes. Meanwhile, put the duck legs in a separate pan, pour over boiling water, and leave for 5 minutes—this will help to remove any blood and excess fat. Drain, then add the duck legs to the red braise and bring back to a boil. Reduce the heat until simmering. Cover the duck with a circle of parchment paper and place a plate on top that just fits inside the pan. This keeps the duck from bobbing up, cooking it evenly (the paper protects the plate from staining). Cook until tender (about 2–2½ hours). Remove the duck legs and set aside.

Strain the duck cooking liquid through a sieve into a large jar or pot. If you are planning on making this in advance, leave the cooking liquid to cool before refrigerating. The next day a layer of fat will have set on the surface. If making immediately, ladle off the fat from the surface and continue with the sauce.

Prepare the mushrooms as follows: shiitakes should be destemmed and quartered; larger oysters torn gently in two (leave smaller oysters whole); and shimejis broken up gently from their clumped base. Heat the oil in a wok and, when hot, add the garlic, shallots, ginger, and chile. Stir-fry for 1 minute or so. Add the mushrooms to the wok, give them a quick stir, then add the duck legs and strained red braising liquid. Simmer for 10 minutes or until the duck legs are hot and the mushrooms are tender.

Stir in the cilantro and pour into deep bowls. Serve with rice topped with Pickled Enoki, Thai basil, and blanched bok choy. Provide some spoons for all that gorgeous liquid!

VARIATIONS

• Make the meal more hearty by adding thin slices of sweet potato or squash while making the sauce.

A delicious warming, fragrant, and fruity curry. If you don't want to make your own curry paste, substitute with 2 tablespoons of Thai red curry paste, or even green, and cook as per the recipe. < SERVES 4 >

#9

DUCK, PINEAPPLE, AND COCONUT CURRY

Lightly score the duck, season with sea salt and pepper and place in a hot, dry pan. Cook over a high heat until browned all over. Pour off any excess fat and set aside.

To make the curry paste, pound or blend all the ingredients together to make a fine paste.

To make the curry, remove the top thick layer of cream from unshaken cans of coconut milk and place this in the wok. When hot, stir in the curry paste and cook for about 2–3 minutes or until fragrant (you are using the coconut "cream" to cook the paste—something I learned in Thailand). Keep stirring, so the paste doesn't burn. Then add the rest of the coconut milk along with 1 cup water and bring to a boil. Add the seared duck and reduce the heat to a simmer. Cover and cook over low heat for about 15 minutes or until the duck is tender. Remove the duck and set aside while you finish the curry.

Skim off any excess fat and add the lime leaves, palm sugar, and pineapple. Simmer for another 10 minutes or until just warmed through. Finish with fish sauce and cilantro.

Slice the duck breasts and divide between four deep bowls. Top with curry sauce and scatter with sliced chile and Thai basil leaves. Serve with lime quarters on the side along with some steamed rice.

VARIATIONS

- Why not create with flavor by introducing some tamarind?
- Omit the pineapple and use lychees instead.
- For a quick dinner, use a pre-cooked Chinese-style duck and warm through in the curry.

4 duck breasts, fat lightly scored

sea salt and black pepper

FOR THE CURRY PASTE
4 red bird's eye chiles
2 shallots, finely sliced
3 garlic cloves, finely chopped
1¼in piece of ginger or galangal, peeled and thinly sliced
2 sticks lemongrass, finely chopped
2 lime leaves, finely chopped
6 cilantro roots, finely chopped (use ½ bunch fresh cilantro if roots unavailable)
1 tbsp coriander seeds, toasted
1 tsp cardamom pods
1 tsp cumin seeds, toasted
1 tsp sea salt
1 tsp green peppercorns, or a little freshly ground pepper

FOR THE CURRY
2 x 14oz cans unsweetened coconut milk
2 lime leaves
2 tbsp palm sugar
1lb 2oz fresh pineapple, diced
2 tbsp fish sauce
½ bunch cilantro, leaves picked
1 green or red chile, finely sliced
handful of Thai basil leaves
1 lime, cut into quarters

27

Sausage rolls are back in fashion! I wanted to cook a version that used some of my favorite Middle Eastern ingredients and take sausage rolls right out of their box!

#10

< MAKES 2 LARGE SAUSAGE ROLLS OR LOTS OF SMALL ONES >

DUCK SAUSAGE ROLLS WITH A TWIST

Preheat the oven to 400°F.

Combine all the filling ingredients and season with sea salt and black pepper. Cook a teaspoon of the mixture to check the seasoning.

Roll the puff pastry out to about ¼in thickness, and cut into two long strips, each about 3in wide. Divide the filling mixture in two and form into a long sausage down the center of each strip of pastry—this should be about ¾in wide and ¾in high.

Brush one edge of each strip with a little water and carefully roll the pastry over the filling to create your sausage rolls. Press the sides together to ensure they are joined. You can either leave the rolls whole or cut into portions as shown in the picture.

Brush each roll with egg and sprinkle with seeds. Arrange on a non-stick baking sheet and cook for 20–25 minutes until golden.

For the salsa, mix all the ingredients together in a small bowl and serve with the sausage rolls.

FOR THE FILLING

1–2 duck legs, meat removed and ground, or ¾lb ground duck

2 garlic cloves, finely chopped

1½ tsp ground cumin

½ tsp ground cinnamon

½ tsp ground coriander

½ tsp paprika

pinch of nutmeg

pinch of ground ginger

1 small red chile, seeded and finely chopped

small bunch cilantro, finely chopped

¼ cup pine nuts, toasted

¼ cup pomegranate molasses

½ Granny Smith apple, grated

1 small carrot, grated

3 Medjool dates, pitted and finely chopped

sea salt and black pepper

1lb 2oz puff pastry

1 egg, beaten, to glaze

2 tbsp sesame seeds, hemp seeds or flax seeds

FOR THE SALSA

7oz cherry tomatoes, chopped

seeds of ½ pomegranate

handful chopped mint leaves

1 carrot, grated

splash of olive oil

splash of red wine vinegar

One of my favorite winter risottos. Italian sausages are made up of pork, spiked with fennel seeds, and have the perfect proportion of fat content. If you can't find them, use cooking chorizo instead. **< SERVES 4—6 >**

ITALIAN SAUSAGE, RED WINE, CHESTNUT, AND CABBAGE RISOTTO

10oz Italian pork sausages
2 tbsp olive oil
4 tbsp unsalted butter
3-4 shallots or 1 onion, finely chopped
2 cups Arborio rice
⅔ cup red wine
2oz cooked chestnuts
2.2 quarts hot chicken stock
9oz shredded cabbage or spring greens, pre-blanched
1 cup Parmesan, finely grated
2–3 tbsp mascarpone
sea salt and black pepper

Remove the skin from the sausages and tear into small pieces. Heat the oil in a pan and cook half the sausage meat until crusty and golden, then drain off the oil and set aside.

Melt the butter in a heavy-bottomed pan, then gently cook the shallots or onion and remaining sausage until softened, but not brown. Add the rice and, using a wooden spoon, toss well until the rice is coated in the buttery shallots and sausage fat. Pour in the wine and allow to evaporate completely before adding the chestnuts and stock.

Add the hot stock to the rice, a ladleful or two at a time, stirring over medium heat until absorbed. After about 15 minutes, add the pre-cooked sausage and the blanched cabbage.

Continue to cook until the rice is *al dente*—about 3 minutes. Turn off the heat, add the Parmesan and mascarpone, season with salt and pepper to taste, and stir through. Serve drizzled with olive oil.

VARIATIONS

- Add some grilled radicchio, doused with a little balsamic vinegar.
- If you're feeling adventurous, try making this risotto with the cooking juices from a slow-braised oxtail. It's divine tossed with the shredded meat and with a squeeze of lemon to cut through the richness.
- Try using peas or soy beans instead of cabbage or spring greens.

Inspired by Nigella's coke-cooked ham, this warming ginger-beer spiced, sticky ham is great for entertaining as it's easily prepared in advance and is sure to wow your guests! < SERVES 8 >

#12

GINGER BEER AND TANGERINE GLAZED HAM

Put the ham, onion, tangerine zest, and star anise in a large saucepan. Pour in the ginger beer and top off with water, if necessary, so that the ham is just covered. Bring to a boil, skim the surface, and reduce the heat to a simmer. Cover and cook for 2–2½ hours, until the meat is tender. Leave to cool in the cooking liquid.

Preheat the oven to 425°F.

Remove the ham from the pan, setting aside the cooking liquid for the lentils. Once cool enough to handle, carefully cut the skin off the ham, making sure to leave a layer of fat. Lightly score the fat into diamond shapes. Line a roasting pan with foil and place the ham on top.

To make the glaze, warm the honey, mustard, and ginger beer in a pan and boil until thickened. Spoon over the fat, then stud a clove into the middle of each diamond and bake for 20–25 minutes or until the glaze has caramelized. (You could prepare the ham in advance and finish in the oven at a later stage; if so, remove from the fridge, bring up to room temperature, cover with glaze, and increase the above cooking time by 10 minutes.)

Leave to cool before slicing. Make sure you skim off the excess fat before using the liquid for the lentils. The best way to do this if you're using immediately is to add a few ice cubes. The fat will congeal and you can ladle the majority off. Alternatively, cool then refrigerate overnight so the fat settles on the top.

4½lb mild-cure ham
1 onion, halved
zest of 4 tangerines, removed with a vegetable peeler (set aside the juice for the lentils)
4 whole star anise
1.9 quarts ginger beer

FOR THE GLAZE
4 tbsp honey
2 tbsp wholegrain mustard
⅓ cup ginger beer
handful of cloves

Chile and Tangerine Braised Lentils, to serve (recipe #53)

VARIATIONS

- Serve hot or cold. Spice it all up with some additional red chile.
- Try poaching a whole chicken or duck in the liquid. Brisket of beef or short ribs would also be great cooked in this way.

35

#13

Overlooked and inexpensive, pork shanks are delicious slow braised with punchy Moroccan spices—ideal for a winter's dinner. Inspired by my Moroccan travels.

< SERVES 4 >

MOROCCAN BRAISED PORK SHANKS

FOR THE SPICE PASTE MARINADE

3 garlic cloves, finely chopped

3 cardamom pods

2 tsp coriander seeds

1½in piece of ginger, grated

pinch of saffron strands

1 tbsp sea salt

1 tbsp ground cumin

1 tbsp sweet paprika

2 tsp chili powder

4 tbsp olive oil

4 small pork hocks, skin removed

FOR THE PORK CASSEROLE

1 onion, diced

2 carrots, diced

1 fennel bulb, diced

1 green chile, seeds removed, finely chopped

1 large cinnamon stick

1 x 14oz can tomatoes, chopped

1 tbsp honey

4 strips orange zest

1 quart chicken stock

1 x 14oz can cooked chickpeas

1 small bunch cilantro, chopped

½ bunch flat-leaf parsley, chopped

1 tbsp mint leaves, chopped

sea salt and black pepper

lemon juice, to taste

Using a mortar and pestle, crush the garlic, cardamom, and coriander seeds with the ginger, saffron, and salt. Add the remaining spices and 2 tablespoons olive oil to form a paste. Rub the paste all over the pork hocks, cover, and chill for several hours (overnight if possible).

Preheat the oven to 375°F.

Heat the remaining olive oil in a roasting pan or casserole dish over medium heat and brown the hocks on all sides. Remove from the pan and set aside.

Add the onion, carrots, fennel, and chile to the pan and cook until lightly colored. Return the ham hocks to the pan, then add the cinnamon, tomatoes, honey, orange zest, and chicken stock. Cover the pan with foil and transfer to the oven.

Cook for 1½–2 hours. Add the chickpeas and cook for another 30 minutes or until the meat is very tender. Remove the hocks and keep warm. Pour the cooking juices into a saucepan and skim off any surface fat. Simmer the sauce until it has reduced by one quarter. Add the fresh herbs and season to taste with salt and pepper. Add a little lemon juice to taste. Serve with couscous.

This gorgeous Tuscan dish is traditionally made using pork loin, but I prefer using pork belly. The slow roasting and aromatic herbs make it deliciously tender and fragrant. The perfect meal for a lazy Sunday. < SERVES 4-6 >

PORCHETTA WITH ROSEMARY ROASTED POTATOES

Preheat the oven to 400°F.

To make the porchetta, lay the pork belly skin-side up on a clean, flat surface. Score the pork fat and remove any excess (a craft knife is perfect for this). Crush the garlic in a large mortar and pestle with a good pinch of sea salt, add the fennel seeds, anchovies, and sage, and bruise.

Transfer to a bowl and add the rosemary, pepper flakes, lemon zest, capers, olive oil, a good grinding of black pepper, and mix. Flip the pork over, so it is skin-side down, then smear the herb and caper mix evenly over it. Set aside to rest for 10 minutes to allow the flavors to develop.

Now you need to carefully roll the meat up widthwise and tie it very tightly in the middle of the belly. Continue to tie at ¾in intervals. If any filling escapes just push it back in! Rub a little oil over the roast and season with some sea salt and pepper. Cut the carrot and onion into quarters, place in a roasting pan, and put the pork on top. The carrot and onion will act as a trivet and stop the pork from sticking to the pan. Roast for 20 minutes, then remove and reduce the oven temperature to 300°F. Add the water or stock, cover with foil and cook for 2½ hours.

Start to prepare the potatoes around 50 minutes before the end of the pork's cooking time. Place the potatoes in a pan, add a pinch of salt, and cover with water. Bring to a boil and simmer for 10 minutes. Pour into a colander, drain, and shake until the potatoes are "fluffy." Heat the oil in a roasting pan, then carefully add the potatoes, season with sea salt, and add the rosemary. Allow the potatoes to color a little in the pan, then shake again.

Remove the pork from the oven and set aside in a warm place to rest. Meanwhile, turn the oven up to 400°F and cook the potatoes for about 25 minutes, until crisp, while resting the pork.

Heat the pork roasting pan on the stove. Scrape off any caramelized pieces and pour the cooking juices into a pitcher. Slice the pork carefully, removing the string, and serve with rosemary roasted potatoes and the pork juices.

FOR THE PORCHETTA

3½lb boneless pork belly

3 garlic cloves

sea salt and black pepper

3 tsp fennel seeds

10 salted anchovies, finely chopped (optional)

½ bunch sage leaves, picked and coarsely chopped

2 sprigs of rosemary, picked and chopped

pinch of crushed red pepper flakes

zest of ½ lemon

2oz capers, rinsed and coarsely chopped

1 tbsp olive oil

1 carrot

1 onion

1 cup stock or water

FOR THE POTATOES

1lb 10oz Yukon Gold potatoes, peeled and cut into 1¼in–1½in pieces

sea salt

4 tbsp olive oil

2 sprigs of rosemary, picked

A quick and easy recipe—comforting and bursting with flavor. Experiment with alternative ingredients by using a different meat and fruit pairing—for example you could try lamb with prunes. < SERVES 4 >

SAUSAGE AND BUTTERNUT SQUASH TAGINE

8 Cumberland or 12 merguez sausages

2 tbsp olive oil

1 small onion, finely chopped

2 garlic cloves, finely chopped

pinch of saffron

3 tsp ground cumin

1 tsp ground ginger

2 tsp paprika

2 tsp coriander seeds, crushed

2 x 14oz cans chopped tomatoes

10½oz butternut squash, peeled and diced into about ¾in cubes

1 red chile, split lengthwise

1 cinnamon stick

2 tbsp honey

sea salt and black pepper

3½oz green pitted olives (optional)

½ preserved lemon, (optional), finely chopped

1oz bunch cilantro, finely chopped

FOR THE COUSCOUS

1¾ cups instant couscous

4 tbsp butter, diced

4 tsp finely grated orange zest

sea salt

4 tsp finely chopped green chiles

chopped cilantro

Remove the skin from the sausages and roll the meat into balls (a little smaller than golf balls).

Heat half the olive oil in a large pan, add the meatballs, and cook over medium heat for about 5 minutes or until browned. Set aside.

Heat the remaining oil and cook the onion gently until softened. Add the garlic and spices and cook for another minute until aromatic.

Stir in the tomatoes, squash, chile, cinnamon stick, and honey, season with salt and pepper, and cook over medium heat for 5 minutes. Add the sausage meatballs and continue to cook for another 25 minutes, adding a little boiling water if the tagine looks a little dry.

While the tagine is cooking, prepare the couscous. Put the couscous, butter, orange zest, and a pinch of salt into a bowl. Pour in 1 cup boiling water, cover the bowl with plastic wrap, and leave for 2–3 minutes to steam. Remove the plastic wrap, fluff up the grains with a fork, and stir in the chile and cilantro.

To serve, stir in the olives and preserved lemon, if using, into the tagine and sprinkle with the chopped cilantro. Accompany with the warm, fluffy couscous.

Anise has a natural affinity for pork. Fennel and fennel seeds accentuate the pork's meatiness and add depth of flavor to complement the rich, slow roasted pork belly. Tomato lifts the flavor with an acidic hit. < SERVES 4 >

#16

SPICED PORK BELLY WITH FENNEL PURÉE AND FENNEL AND TOMATO SALAD

Preheat the oven to 425°F.

Place the pork on a work surface, skin-side up, and use a clean craft knife to score lines into the pork rind, about ½in apart. Cut through the skin into the fat, but not into the meat. (You can ask your butcher to do this for you.) Mix together the fennel and coriander seeds, 1 tablespoon sea salt, and the paprika. Rub this all over the skin, pushing it deep into the scored fat. Place the vegetables and thyme in a roasting pan and place the pork on top, skin-side up. Add half the stock and place in the oven. Roast for about 30 minutes, until the skin of the pork has started to turn into crackling.

Meanwhile, prepare the fennel for the purée. Cut the bulbs in half lengthwise, then remove and discard the outer layer and core. Place the fennel and garlic on a piece of foil, drizzle with half the oil, sprinkle with salt, and form a loose parcel. Place on a baking sheet. When the pork has been in for half an hour, reduce the heat to 350°F. Add the remaining liquid to the meat and place the fennel parcel on another shelf in the oven. Roast for a further 1½ hours.

Remove the pork from the oven and rest for 10 minutes. Pass the juices through a fine sieve and skim off any excess fat.

Place the cooked fennel and garlic in a blender. Add the lemon juice, the rest of the olive oil, and 2 tablespoons pork cooking liquid. Blend until smooth, then season to taste.

While the pork is resting, make the salad. Cut the fennel in half lengthwise, then remove and discard the outer layer and core. Thinly slice the bulb horizontally. Place in a bowl with the tomatoes and any wispy fennel tops. Crush the garlic with 1 teaspoon sea salt. Whisk the garlic, vinegar, and oils together and pour over salad, tossing with some salt and pepper.

Cut the pork lengthwise into about ¾in strips and serve on top of the purée, with the salad.

2¼lb boneless pork belly, skin on
2 tbsp fennel seeds
1 tbsp coriander seeds
1 tbsp sea salt
2 tsp sweet smoked paprika
2 carrots, peeled and halved lengthwise
2 celery ribs, halved
1 onion, cut into thin wedges
4 garlic cloves, unpeeled
few sprigs of fresh thyme
2½ cups chicken stock

FOR THE PURÉE
2 fennel bulbs
1 garlic clove
2 tbsp olive oil
sea salt
juice of ½ lemon

FOR THE SALAD
1 fennel bulb
7oz cherry vine tomatoes, halved
3½oz yellow cherry vine tomatoes, halved
1 garlic clove
sea salt
4 tsp red wine vinegar
8 tsp olive oil
1 bunch watercress, picked into sprigs

41

A childhood favorite—lamb meatballs combined with a hint of spice, gently cooked with petit pois, tomatoes, and unconventional mashed potatoes makes this a super cozy sofa dinner. < SERVES 4 >

COZY LAMB MEATBALLS WITH PEAS AND TOMATO SAUCE

FOR THE MEATBALLS
1lb 2oz ground lamb
2 garlic cloves, crushed
pinch of cayenne pepper
2 tsp ground cumin
1 tsp ground cinnamon
1 tsp paprika
1 tsp turmeric
flour, for dusting
4 tbsp olive oil

**FOR THE PEA AND
TOMATO SAUCE**
2 tbsp olive oil
1 small onion, finely chopped
2 garlic cloves, finely chopped
1 tbsp tomato paste
1 tsp ground cinnamon
1 x 14oz can plum
tomatoes, crushed
pinch of sugar
1 chicken bouillon cube
3½oz frozen petit pois
1 tbsp dried dill
sea salt
½ bunch mint, finely chopped

To make the meatballs, simply mix all the ingredients except the flour and oil together and form into balls. Dust the balls in flour. Heat half the oil in a frying pan and add the meatballs. Cook over medium heat for 5 minutes. Cook until the meatballs are medium-rare in the center (about 3 minutes, depending on the size). Then set aside and repeat with the remaining oil and meatballs.

For the sauce, heat the oil in a saucepan and gently cook the onion and garlic until softened. Add the tomato paste and cinnamon and cook for a couple more minutes. Add the tomatoes and sugar and crumble in the bouillon cube. Bring to a boil, then simmer for 5 minutes. Add the peas and dill along with ⅔ cup water and cook for 15 minutes over low heat. Add the meatballs and cook for another 15 minutes, adding a little boiling water if the sauce is a little thick. Season with sea salt, stir in the mint, and serve with mashed potatoes.

VARIATIONS

- Serve with flatbread and sprinkle with crumbled feta.
- For an Asian twist, swap the meatball spices for ground ginger, cumin, coriander, a pinch of crushed red pepper flakes, and turmeric. Omit the cinnamon and the dried dill from the sauce and add some freshly chopped ginger, then finish with chopped cilantro and lemongrass.

44

My neighbor and I have an annual summer barbecue. We often get emails from friends asking when it will be so they can plan their vacations around it! This recipe is one of the main reasons they show up. < SERVES 4–6 >

DILL AND LEMON MARINATED LAMB

3 garlic cloves

3 tbsp sea salt

1 bunch dill, finely chopped, with stems

6 tbsp olive oil

zest and juice of 2 lemons

2¼lb boneless leg of lamb, cut into muscle steaks (follow the natural seams in the boneless joint and cut into pieces—you will probably end up with about 4)

Lemon and Dill Braised Fava Beans (recipe #70), to serve (optional)

Pound the garlic and sea salt in a mortar and pestle to form a paste. Transfer to a bowl and mix with the dill, olive oil, lemon zest, and juice.

Trim each lamb steak of excess fat and remove any visible sinew. Smear the garlic paste all over the lamb and leave to marinate for at least 3 hours or, preferably, overnight in the refrigerator.

Bring the lamb back up to room temperature before cooking to ensure it cooks evenly.

Preheat a grill pan or outdoor grill. Drain and lift the meat out of the marinade and shake off and set aside any excess. Place on the grill pan or grill and cook for about 5 minutes on each side. You can use the excess marinade to baste the lamb while it's cooking.

Set the lamb aside for 10 minutes to rest before slicing. Serve warm with Lemon and Dill Braised Fava Beans.

VARIATIONS

- This is also delicious served with flatbread and Greek yogurt or labneh.
- Create new flavors by varying the marinade ingredients—oregano also complements lemon, as do tarragon and mint.

Three of my favorite ingredients in one hit: lamb, feta, and watermelon. Juicy medium-rare lamb is marinated in earthy cinnamon with a touch of oregano (keeping it Greek). The dukkah spice mix adds crunch. < SERVES 4 >

DUKKAH ROLLED LAMB, FETA MINT CURD, WATERMELON, AND OLIVES

Combine the marinade ingredients, rub all over the lamb loins, and leave to marinate for at least 30 minutes, or overnight in the refrigerator. Remove from the fridge 30 minutes before cooking, allowing it to come back to room temperature.

Preheat the oven to 400°F.

Season the lamb fillets with sea salt, preheat a ridged grill pan and, once hot, brown the fillets all over. Transfer to a baking sheet and roast for 6 minutes, until cooked but still pink. Remove from the oven.

Sprinkle some dukkah on a plate and roll each fillet to coat. Cover loosely with foil and leave to rest for 10 minutes before carving into ¼in slices.

To make the feta mint curd, place the yogurt, feta, and garlic in a food processor. Blend until smooth, then drizzle in the olive oil, stir in the mint, and refrigerate until required. You can make this the day before.

To serve, spread the feta mint curd over the watermelon, top with olives and arugula, and place the sliced lamb on top. Whisk together the oil and Cabernet Sauvignon vinegar and drizzle over the lamb. Serve immediately.

VARIATIONS

- This is equally delicious with a piece of rare tuna (no need to marinate). It's up to you whether you want to include the dukkah.
- For a vegetarian version, roll the watermelon in the dukkah and top with feta mint curd, olives, arugula, tomatoes, cooked chickpeas, and some chopped scallions.

FOR THE MARINADE
zest of 1 lemon
2 tbsp olive oil
3 tbsp honey
2 sprigs of oregano, leaves picked and finely chopped
1 tsp ground cinnamon
2 garlic cloves, crushed
8 tbsp Dukkah (recipe #58)

FOR THE LAMB
4 lamb loin fillets (6oz each), trimmed
sea salt

FOR THE FETA MINT CURD
½ cup Greek yogurt
1⅓ cups feta cheese, crumbled
1 garlic clove, crushed
1 tbsp extra virgin olive oil
2 tbsp chopped mint

TO SERVE
seedless watermelon, chilled and cut into 4 blocks 6in long, 2in wide, and ¾in deep
2½oz pitted Kalamata olives, coarsely chopped
small handful of arugula
3 tbsp extra virgin olive oil
2 tbsp Cabernet Sauvignon vinegar (if unavailable, use red wine vinegar)

Add a new dimension to a Sunday roast. Shoulder of lamb is an economical cut and is just right for slow roasting: minimum preparation that produces maximum results! You'll need some butcher's twine for this recipe. < SERVES 6–8 >

SLOW-ROASTED SHOULDER OF LAMB WITH FENNEL SAUSAGE STUFFING

To make the stuffing, heat half the oil in a frying pan, add the onion and garlic, and sauté over low heat until it begins to caramelize (10–15 minutes). Remove from the heat and transfer to a bowl. Add the fennel seeds and pepper flakes and stir in the bread crumbs. Leave to cool. Add the sausage meat, season with sea salt and pepper, and mix well.

Preheat the oven to 400°F.

Place the lamb skin-side down on a board and season with sea salt and black pepper. Spread over the stuffing, roll up tightly, secure with twine, and place in a roasting pan with 1 cup water. Rub with the remaining oil and season. Roast for 20 minutes, then reduce the heat to 350°F and cook for 1½–2 hours, basting occasionally with any juices. Remove the lamb from the oven, cover with foil, and leave to rest for at least 20 minutes.

For the wilted greens, halve the fennel lengthwise, remove the core, and slice across as thinly as possible. Heat half the oil in a large frying pan, add the fennel and garlic, and cook until tender. Set aside. Return the pan to the heat and add a dash more oil, plus half the mixed greens. Leave to wilt a little, toss with salt and pepper, and set aside. Repeat with the remaining greens, then return the cooked greens and fennel to the pan, adjust the seasoning, and stir in the lemon juice.

Remove the twine from the lamb and carve into slices. Serve with the wilted greens and drizzle with the lamb cooking juices.

1 boneless shoulder of lamb, 3¾–4½lb

FOR THE STUFFING
4 tbsp olive oil
1 onion, finely chopped
2 garlic cloves, finely chopped
2 tsp fennel seeds
pinch of crushed red pepper flakes
1⅔ cups fresh bread crumbs
1lb 2oz fennel or merguez sausages, skins removed
sea salt and black pepper

FOR THE WILTED GREENS
2 fennel bulbs
4 tbsp olive oil
2 garlic cloves
2¼lb mixed green leaves (such as spinach, arugula, dandelion, and chard)
sea salt and black pepper
juice of 1 lemon

VARIATIONS

• Delicious served with Warm Chickpea Purée (recipe #104), or Spinach with Garlic, Raisins, and Pine Nuts (recipe #69) instead of wilted greens.

This dish takes me right back to my childhood, as my mom used to make it frequently. It's a delicious way to prepare lamb, inspired by my dad's Greek Cypriot way of braising meat in a rich, tomatoey sauce. < SERVES 4 >

BRAISED LAMB LOIN WITH RUNNER BEANS AND TOMATOES

3 garlic cloves, finely chopped

2 tsp sea salt

zest of ½ lemon

4 tbsp olive oil

2¼lb lamb loin, on the bone or chops

1 onion, finely chopped

1 celery rib, finely chopped

4 tsp tomato paste

6 fresh tomatoes, peeled and coarsely chopped, or 1 x 14oz can plum tomatoes, chopped

1 quart chicken stock

½ tsp sea salt and black pepper

1 fresh bay leaf

1¼in cinnamon stick

1lb medium-sized potatoes, peeled and quartered

4 tbsp parsley, chopped

2 tbsp dill, chopped

10½oz runner beans, sliced

Crush 2 of the garlic cloves with 2 teaspoons of sea salt to form a paste. Mix with lemon zest and half the olive oil and rub all over the lamb. Marinate for 1 hour or overnight.

Heat the remaining olive oil in a pan large enough to hold the lamb and potatoes. Once hot, brown the lamb in batches and set aside.

Add the onion, remaining garlic, and the celery to the pan and cook until softened before adding the tomato paste. Cook for another minute, before adding the tomatoes and chicken stock. Bring to a boil and season with salt and pepper. Add the bay leaf, cinnamon stick, and the lamb. Cover and simmer for 1 hour.

Now add the potatoes and simmer for 20 minutes uncovered before adding half the parsley, the dill, and the runner beans. Simmer for another 15 minutes, until the beans and potatoes are tender.

Serve in deep bowls, sprinkled with the remaining parsley. This dish tastes even better the day after it's made.

slow-braise to tenderize until it melts in the mouth — mmmm

has an open, grainy texture

...and the cow

BRISKET

take it on an Asian adventure — braise in ginger, garlic, warming cinnamon, star anise, chile, soy sauce, shaoxing, and dried orange peel

forgotten cuts

oxtail

beef cheeks

= one aromatic, mouth-watering, delicious dinner of melting beef

I love tangy flavors and a bit of spice

LUCKY COW!

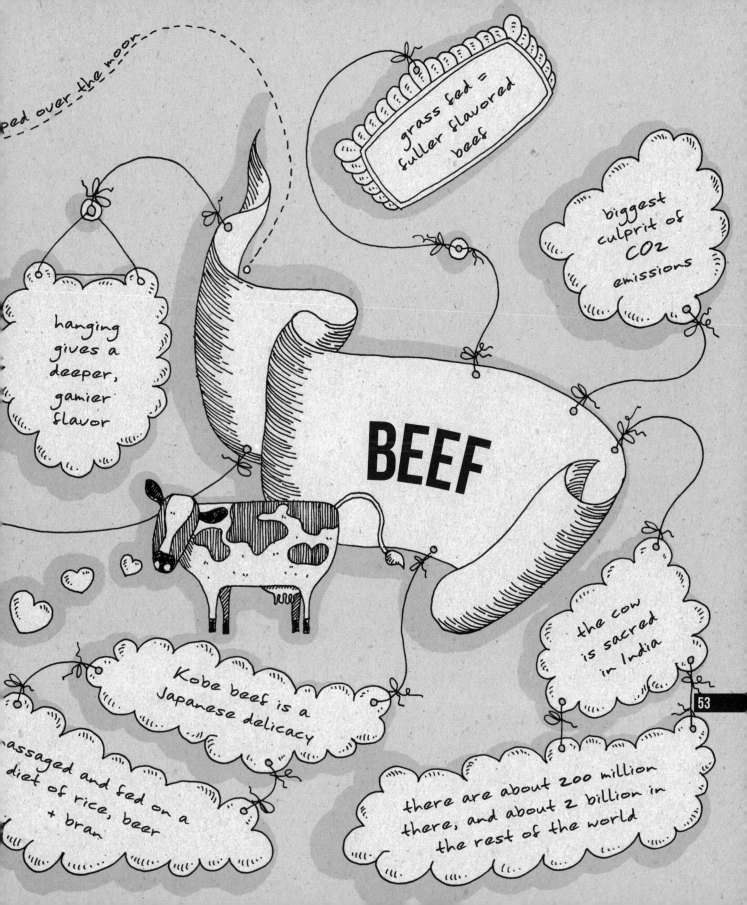

The combination of veal chops with creamy sage and onion polenta is just sublime! A hint of sweetness from the quince along with sharpness from the Manchego bring this whole dish together. < SERVES 4 >

VEAL CHOP TOPPED WITH MELTED MANCHEGO AND QUINCE, WITH CREAMY SAGE AND ONION POLENTA

Crush the garlic and thyme in a mortar and pestle, mix with the olive oil and lemon zest, and rub all over the veal chops. Marinate for 30 minutes or refrigerate overnight.

For the polenta, remove the stems from the sage leaves and set aside; finely chop the leaves. Melt the butter in a large saucepan and add the onions and sage leaves. Cook over low heat for about 30 minutes, or until the onions are soft and caramelized.

Meanwhile, heat the milk, 1⅔ cups water, and the reserved sage stems together. Once hot, fish out the sage stems and discard. Add the nutmeg and slowly whisk in the polenta; cook according to package instructions over low heat, stirring constantly until thickened. You may need to add a little more hot water if the polenta seems too thick.

Remove from the heat and stir in the caramelized onions and mascarpone, seasoning to taste. Keep this warm while you are preparing the chops.

Preheat a ridged grill pan, season the chops, and cook over medium heat for 4–5 minutes on each side, depending on their thickness.

Top the chops with the slices of membrillo and Manchego and scatter with plenty of cracked black pepper and some thyme leaves. Place under a preheated broiler or in the oven for 1–2 minutes, until golden and bubbling. Divide the polenta between four plates, place a chop on each, and serve.

2 garlic cloves
3 tsp thyme leaves, plus
1 tsp for garnish
3 tbsp olive oil
finely grated zest of 1 lemon
4 veal chops
4½oz membrillo (quince paste), thinly sliced
4½oz Manchego cheese, thinly sliced
cracked black pepper

FOR THE POLENTA
20 sage leaves, finely chopped and stalks reserved
7 tbsp butter
3½ cups onions, thinly sliced
1⅔ cups milk
pinch of nutmeg
2 cups instant polenta
3½oz mascarpone
sea salt and black pepper

VARIATION

- Try topping the veal with a blue cheese, such as *blu di capra* (a delicate blue goat cheese from Italy) instead of Manchego.

I'm such a snob when it comes to burgers, I'll admit. If I'm going to eat a burger, it's got to be top quality. I think this hits the mark for a great alternative to the traditional beef burger. < SERVES 4 >

VITELLO TONNATO BURGER

FOR THE BURGERS

1½lb best-quality
ground veal

1 shallot, finely diced

2oz capers, rinsed and coarsely
chopped

zest of 1 lemon

a handful of flat-leaf
parsley, finely chopped

drizzle of olive oil

sea salt and black pepper

4 ciabatta rolls, halved

1 bunch watercress, picked

FOR THE TONNATO SAUCE

2 egg yolks

2 tbsp lemon juice

5 salted anchovy fillets,
finely chopped

¾ cup olive oil

7oz canned sustainable tuna in
olive oil, drained

1 tbsp salted capers, rinsed

splash of white wine vinegar

squeeze of lemon juice

FOR THE CRISPY CAPERS

3 tbsp olive oil

2 tbsp capers, rinsed and dried

To make the burgers, mix together the veal, shallots, capers, lemon zest, parsley, and olive oil. Season with pepper and a little salt (not too much—the capers are salty). Taste for seasoning—if you don't want to try the mix raw, cook off a teaspoon or so and then taste. Divide the mixture into four and shape into balls. Refrigerate for up to 1 hour. Shape into burgers about 2–2½in in diameter.

To make the sauce, whisk together the egg yolks, lemon juice, and anchovies in a food processor until smooth. Then, with the motor running, add the oil in a thin, steady stream. You can also do this by hand with a whisk. Add half the tuna and the capers. Pulse, just enough to combine, then fold through the remaining tuna. (If making by hand you may want to coarsely chop the tuna and capers to break them down a little). Finish by whisking in a little vinegar and lemon juice to taste. Chill until required—the sauce will keep for up to three days in the refrigerator. (Note: traditionally, the sauce would be made with some of the veal cooking liquid and would use hard-boiled eggs. However, since the vitello in this case is a burger, we don't have any liquid! I apologize to all vitello tonnato purists out there.)

For the crispy capers, heat the oil in a small pan. Once hot, carefully add the capers and cook over medium heat until crisp (1–2 minutes). Remove from the pan and drain on paper towels.

To cook the burgers, preheat a grill pan or outdoor grill. Drizzle with olive oil and cook for 2–3 minutes on either side, depending on your taste preference.

Drizzle the ciabatta rolls with olive oil and lightly toast, then spread with tonnato sauce, layer with some watercress, and top with a burger. Garnish with crispy capers, if using. Serve with extra sauce on the side.

I was introduced to Asian braising by my talented chef friend Kim. So underrated, slow-braised brisket produces mouth-watering results. Hopefully a recipe that will stay in your repertoire for a long time. < SERVES 4–6 >

ASIAN BRAISED BRISKET OF BEEF

1 piece brisket of beef, about 3½lb

FOR THE BRAISE
¾ cup yellow rock sugar (use palm sugar if unavailable)
1½in piece of fresh ginger, sliced
3 garlic cloves, peeled
2 red chiles, halved lengthwise
2 cinnamon sticks
4 star anise
¾ cup soy sauce
¾ cup Shaoxing (use sherry if unavailable)
2 shallots, halved
2 pieces dried orange peel

FOR THE BRISKET SAUCE
2 tbsp peanut oil
2 shallots, finely chopped
1¼in piece of fresh ginger, finely chopped
1 red chile, finely chopped
1 garlic clove, finely chopped
6 cilantro roots, finely chopped
¼ cup yellow rock sugar

TO SERVE
2 tbsp chopped cilantro
1 red chile, finely sliced
jasmine rice and broccoli or bok choy

Place the brisket in a large pan of cold water, bring to a boil, and then refresh under cold running water. Blanching the brisket like this removes the "scum." The brisket is now ready for braising.

Place all the ingredients for the braise in a large pot with 2½ quarts water and bring to a boil. Simmer for 20 minutes before adding the beef. Bring to a boil again then simmer, cover with parchment paper, and weigh down with a plate that just fits inside the pan. This stops the brisket from bobbing up, cooking it evenly (the paper protects the plate from staining). Continue to cook for 2–3 hours until very tender. Remove the beef and set aside. Skim the fat from the surface and pass the stock through a fine sieve. Leave to cool.

For the sauce, heat the peanut oil in a saucepan, add the shallots, ginger, chile, garlic, and cilantro roots, and cook until softened. Add the sugar and 2⅓ cups of the reserved braising liquid and bring to a boil. Reduce the heat and simmer until reduced by two-thirds.

Slice the beef into ¾in steaks and serve on deep plates, topped with ladles of sauce and sprinkled with cilantro and red chile, if desired. Serve with jasmine rice and broccoli or bok choy.

While watching early-morning TV in a hotel in Sydney, I saw an amazing meatloaf being cooked. I raced out of bed, grabbed a pen and paper, and scribbled down as much as I could. Here's my version. < SERVES 4 (VERY GENEROUSLY) >

MEATLOAF

Preheat the oven to 350°F.

Cut a large piece of parchment paper and place on a work surface. Place a 8½ x 4½in loaf or terrine pan on top and pen mark the length of the pan on the paper.

Lay the prosciutto slices on the parchment paper, overlapping them so as to fill the length of the pan without any gaps. Place the mint leaves on top, then lay the salami or chorizo slices down the center.

Place the ground meats in a large bowl and mix with the onion, garlic, cheeses, bread crumbs, and herbs. Season with sea salt and black pepper.

Whisk together the mustard, eggs, Worcestershire, brown, and sweet chili sauces and pour over the meat. Mix until well combined. (I like to cook off a little at this stage, so I can check the mix for seasoning before cooking.)

Place the meat mixture (there is a lot of it, but don't be concerned) on top of the salami slices and shape into a sausage. Using the parchment paper to help you, roll the meatloaf up into a tight roll. Discard the parchment paper and lay the bacon slices on top of the roll.

Lay a large piece of plastic wrap on the work surface and overlay with six more large pieces of plastic wrap, each one slightly overlapping the last so as to form a large, thick piece of wrap that will encase the meatloaf. Place the meatloaf on top and roll up. Twist the ends in opposite directions and tie to secure. Slide the whole thing into the terrine or loaf pan, and then place that in a roasting pan. Pour about 1½in boiling water into the roasting pan and place in the oven (you are not cooking the meatloaf with direct heat so don't worry about leaving the plastic wrap on!). Cook for 1½–1¾ hours.

To check if the meatloaf is done, place a skewer into the center, press down to release the juices, and make sure that they run clear. Remove from the oven and leave to cool for 30 minutes before transferring to a cutting board. Cut one end of the plastic wrap and pour the juices into a small bowl. Cut away the plastic wrap and slice the meatloaf. Serve with creamy mashed potatoes and a fresh tomato sauce.

8 slices of prosciutto

12 mint leaves

4 slices salami or chorizo

1lb 2oz ground beef

9oz ground pork

9oz ground veal (substitute with more ground pork, if you wish)

1 large onion, finely chopped or grated

2 garlic cloves, finely chopped

1¾ cups applewood-smoked Cheddar, grated

⅓ cup Parmesan, finely grated

2¼ cups fresh bread crumbs

1 tsp dried mint

2 tsp fresh thyme leaves

handful of flat-leaf parsley, finely chopped

sea salt and black pepper

1 tbsp Dijon mustard

2 eggs

1 tbsp Worcestershire sauce

2 tbsp steak sauce

2 tbsp sweet chili sauce or ketchup

6 slices thick-cut bacon

This dish brings back fond memories of my time spent working in Tuscany. Tagliata literally means "to slice." In Tuscany, they usually make this with sirloin or tenderloin; personally, I think rib eye works just as well. <SERVES 4>

TAGLIATA WITH GREEN TOMATOES, OREGANO, AND MUSTARD

To prepare the tomatoes, slice them ½in thick. Gently heat the olive oil in a large frying pan, remove from heat, add the garlic, and allow to warm through. Return the pan to the heat and add the tomatoes. Season with sea salt and cook over low heat for 10 minutes. Add the remaining ingredients and simmer for another 10–15 minutes, or until the tomatoes have softened but still hold their shape. They should be sweet, but slightly sour. You may need to do this in batches depending on how large your frying pan is.

To prepare the steaks, drizzle them with olive oil and mix together some salt, pepper, and the rosemary and rub over the meat.

Preheat a ridged grill pan and briskly sear the steaks on either side for 2–3 minutes for a medium-rare result. Set aside to rest before slicing.

To serve, place the tomatoes on either individual plates or a large serving dish. Toss the arugula with the olive oil and place on top of the tomatoes. Slice the steak diagonally into ¾in pieces and loosely arrange over the arugula. Serve immediately, with shaved Parmesan, if desired.

14oz green tomatoes (about 2 large), cores removed

3 tbsp olive oil

2 garlic cloves, finely chopped

sea salt

3 tsp chopped oregano leaves

pinch of crushed red pepper flakes

2–4 tbsp demerara sugar, to taste

3 tbsp Savora mustard (if unavailable, use 1½ tsp Dijon mustard)

¼ cup white wine or cider vinegar

FOR THE STEAKS

2 rib-eye steaks, about 10oz each and ¾in thick

dash of olive oil

sea salt and black pepper

leaves of 1 sprig of rosemary, finely chopped

2 handfuls of arugula

shaved Parmesan (optional)

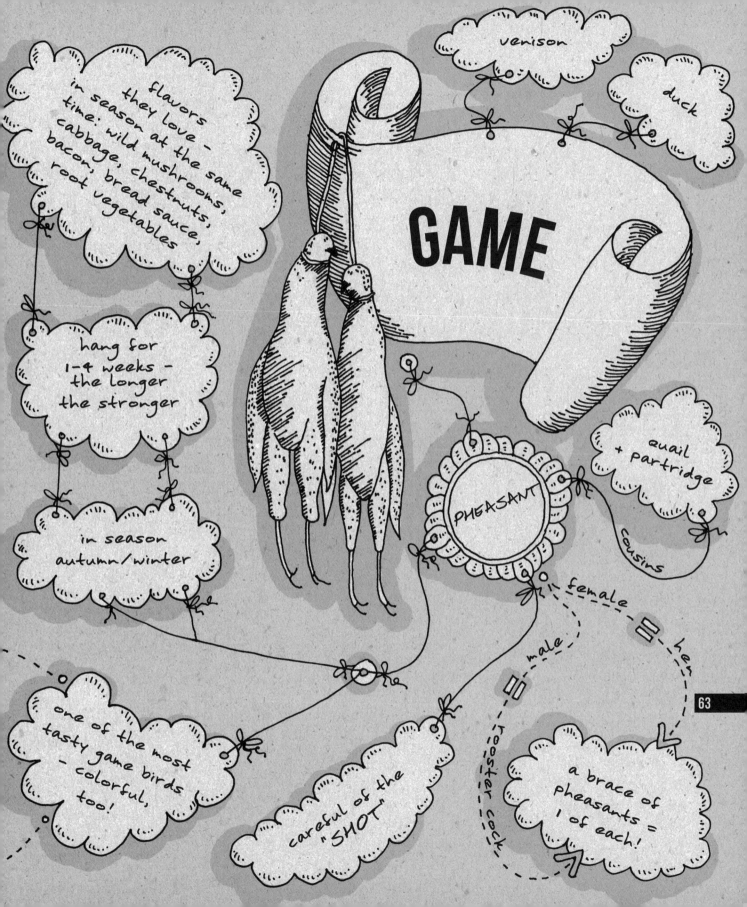

GAME

venison

duck

flavors they love – in season at the same time: wild mushrooms, cabbage, chestnuts, bacon, bread sauce, root vegetables

hang for 1-4 weeks – the longer the stronger

in season autumn/winter

PHEASANT

quail + partridge

cousins

female — her

male

rooster cock

one of the most tasty game birds – colorful, too!

careful of the "SHOT"

a brace of pheasants = 1 of each!

This traditional Tuscan soup is almost a stew; and since I'm not a traditionalist, I've added rabbit! If you have time, try to make the soup a day ahead to allow the flavors to infuse. < SERVES 4—6 >

RABBIT RIBOLLITA

good dash of olive oil

2 rabbit legs

sea salt and black pepper

1½ cups dried cannellini beans, soaked in cold water overnight and drained

1 bay leaf

2 small onions

2 celery ribs

2 carrots

2 garlic cloves, finely chopped

pinch of crushed red pepper flakes

2 heaping tbsp tomato paste

1 rind of Parmesan

14oz plum vine tomatoes, peeled and chopped

1 bunch Swiss chard, leaves coarsely chopped or 10½oz cavolo nero leaves, torn

4 slices ciabatta

extra virgin olive oil

shaved or grated Parmesan, to serve

In a large pan, heat a little of the olive oil, season the rabbit legs with salt and pepper, and sear on both sides until golden. Add the cannellini beans, bay leaf, and enough water to cover. Add half an onion, 1 celery rib and 1 carrot chopped in half. Bring to a boil, reduce to a simmer, and cook for 1 hour or until the beans and rabbit legs are both tender. Drain, setting aside the cooking liquid and discarding the bay leaf and vegetables. Meanwhile, finely chop the remaining onions, celery and carrot.

Heat the remaining oil in a large pan. Add the chopped vegetables, garlic, and pepper flakes and cook over low heat until tender, for about 15–20 minutes. Add the tomato paste and cook for 2 minutes, stirring over medium heat. Add the beans, Parmesan rind, and tomatoes along with 1 quart of the reserved cooking liquid; bring back to a boil and then simmer for another 20 minutes. Meanwhile, tear the meat from the rabbit legs and shred by hand. Set aside.

Remove the Parmesan rind and place in a blender along with a quarter of the soup and blend to a smooth purée. Return to the pan along with the chard or cavolo nero leaves and cook for another 20 minutes.

Season to taste with salt and pepper. The consistency should be stew like; if too thick, add a little more cooking liquid.

Drizzle the ciabatta slices with olive oil and cook on a grill pan on each side until golden. Divide the rabbit meat between preheated bowls, ladle over the hot soup, and top with ciabatta, Parmesan, and a healthy drizzle of olive oil.

VARIATIONS

- If rabbit's not your thing, use pancetta instead—cut into cubes and cook with the vegetables. Chorizo would also be a great alternative.

Gamey rabbit, succulent figs, and rich flavorful porcinis: Oh my gosh, a feast for your senses on one plate! Rabbit is an underused meat that makes a great alternative to chicken. < SERVES 4 >

CHICKEN LIVER STUFFED RABBIT WITH PORCINI BRAISED BARLEY

FOR THE STUFFING
5 tbsp sweet sherry
or vin santo
3½oz dried figs, *finely chopped*
4 tbsp olive oil
2 tsp fennel seeds
3 shallots, *finely chopped*
2 garlic cloves, *finely chopped*
1oz pancetta, *finely chopped*
4 sage leaves, *finely chopped*
1lb 2oz chicken livers
sea salt and black pepper
¼ cup bread crumbs

1 whole rabbit, *deboned*
sea salt and black pepper
2 tbsp olive oil
1 carrot, *coarsely chopped*
1 onion, *coarsely chopped*
1 celery rib, *coarsely chopped*
2⅓ cups chicken or rabbit stock
⅓ cup white or red wine

FOR THE PORCINI BRAISED BARLEY
1 quart chicken stock
1oz dried porcini
4 tbsp butter
2 shallots, *finely chopped*
1 cup pearl barley
1 cup red or white wine

Preheat the oven to 400°F.

First make the stuffing. Heat the sherry or vin santo in a small pan and then pour it over the figs. Leave to soak. Heat half the olive oil in a large frying pan, add the fennel seeds, shallots, garlic, pancetta, and sage and cook until softened and lightly colored. Transfer to a bowl and leave to cool. Heat the remaining oil and add the chicken livers. Season and cook for 2 minutes until browned. Remove from the heat and leave to cool.

Place the livers in a food processor with the shallot mixture, figs, and bread crumbs and pulse until just combined. If you don't have a food processor, finely chop the livers and mix by hand. Season.

Place the rabbit skin-side down on a work surface. Season the cavity. Spread the stuffing evenly over the rabbit. Fold the belly over the stuffing to close, then fold the front and back legs over to form a parcel. Tie with butcher's twine to secure. Heat the olive oil in a small roasting pan. Once hot, sear the rabbit on both sides until golden, then turn off the heat and remove the rabbit. Add the carrot, onion, and celery to the pan. Place the rabbit on top and pour in the stock and wine. Place in the oven and cook for 1½ hours, basting every 20 minutes.

Meanwhile, make the porcini braised barley. Heat the stock and pour over the dried mushrooms. In a separate saucepan, heat the butter and cook the shallots gently until softened. Add the barley and cook for a minute, stirring constantly. Add the wine and cook until absorbed. Pour over the hot stock and mushrooms, bring to a boil, reduce the heat, and simmer for 40–60 minutes, stirring occasionally, until the barley is tender and the liquid has been absorbed. Season to taste.

Remove the rabbit from the oven and leave to rest for 10–15 minutes before removing the twine and carving into ¾in-thick slices. Meanwhile, strain the cooking liquid into a small pan, discard the vegetables, and reduce to thicken. Skim and discard the fat and spoon the liquid over the rabbit. Serve the rabbit and its cooking juices with the porcini braised barley.

It's more economical to buy a whole bird, and the next two recipes offer ideas for using the legs and the breasts. The roast pheasant breast goes beautifully with the Pheasant, Prune, and Bacon Rolls (recipe #30). <SERVES 4>

ROAST PHEASANT BREAST WITH HERBED PUY LENTILS AND CELERIAC CREAM

Rinse the lentils and place in a saucepan. Cover with cold water and bring to a boil. Simmer and cook until tender (about 20–35 minutes), then drain. Heat the olive oil in a saucepan, add the vegetables, and simmer until softened. Add the drained lentils, sherry vinegar, and herbs and season to taste. Keep the lentils warm.

To make the celeriac cream, place the celeriac, cream, and ⅔ cup water in a saucepan with a pinch of sea salt. Bring to a simmer and cook gently for 20–25 minutes, until the celeriac is soft. Add the butter and process in a blender while hot to a smooth purée. Season again with salt and black pepper and keep warm.

Preheat the oven to 400°F.

Heat the oil and butter in an ovenproof frying pan. Season the pheasant breasts with sea salt and pepper, then cook them skin-side down over medium–high heat until golden.

Turn the pheasant breasts over, sprinkle with thyme, and add the wine or sherry. Heat until bubbling, then transfer to the oven and roast for 10–12 minutes or until the juices run clear when the breasts are pierced with a knife. Remove from the pan, add the cooking juices to the lentils, and leave to rest in a warm place for 8–10 minutes before serving.

Serve the the roast pheasant breast with the lentils and celeriac cream.

VARIATIONS

- I like to serve this dish scattered with a few roasted hazelnuts too—they go beautifully with celeriac and prunes.

FOR THE HERBED PUY LENTILS
1 cup puy lentils

2 tbsp olive oil

2 shallots, finely chopped

1 carrot, finely chopped

1 celery rib, finely chopped

4 tbsp sherry vinegar

2 tbsp mixed chopped herbs (such as chives, chervil, and flat-leaf parsley)

sea salt and black pepper

FOR THE CELERIAC CREAM
2 cups celeriac, cut into about ¾in dice

¾ cup heavy cream

sea salt and black pepper

2 tbsp unsalted butter, diced

2 tbsp olive oil

1 tbsp unsalted butter

4 pheasant breasts

2 tsp thyme leaves, picked

⅓ cup white wine or sherry

Two recipes in one: you confit the pheasant legs a day ahead, then use the flaked meat to make the rolls. Pheasant has a natural affinity for prunes—a little sweetness to pep up the gamey confit flavor. < SERVES 8 >

PHEASANT, PRUNE, AND BACON ROLLS

Mix together the coarse salt, peppercorns, thyme, bay leaves, garlic, juniper berries, and orange zest to make confit salt. Scatter half the mixture on the bottom of a non-reactive container, place the pheasant legs on top, and scatter with the remaining mixture. Cover and refrigerate for 12 hours but no longer!

Preheat the oven to 250°F. Select an ovenproof dish that will hold the legs and fat snugly. Put the duck fat in the dish and warm over low heat until dissolved.

Rinse the pheasant legs of salt and pat dry. Submerge into the duck fat and then heat to a gentle simmer.

Cover the surface directly with parchment paper, then cover the dish with foil. Cook in the oven for about 1 hour or until the meat is tender.

Leave the legs to cool in the fat. Remove and flake the meat from the bones, strain the fat, and reserve for another use. If making ahead of time, store the pheasant in a clean container covered with fat and refrigerate until required.

When you're ready to make the rolls, preheat the oven to 400°F. Heat the olive oil in a pan, add the shallots, and cook until softened. Transfer to a bowl and mix with the herbs, pheasant and sausage meat, nutmeg, prunes, and duck fat. Season with sea salt and black pepper—cook off a little of the mixture to check the seasoning.

Shape into 1oz lozenges and wrap each "sausage" in half a slice of bacon. Place on a non-stick baking sheet and cook in the oven for 12–15 minutes, until golden and cooked through.

VARIATION

- If you prefer, you can serve the confit pheasant legs whole and skip making the rolls. Shake off excess fat and place on a baking sheet. Roast in the oven for 10–15 minutes at 350°F, until the skin is crisp and golden, and serve with celeriac cream and lentils (see recipe #29).

FOR THE CONFIT PHEASANT LEGS
½ cup coarse sea salt
1 tsp black peppercorns
3 sprigs of thyme, picked
2 bay leaves, coarsely chopped
2 cloves garlic, thinly sliced
3 juniper berries, crushed
3 strips of orange zest
4 pheasant legs
10½oz duck fat

2 tbsp olive oil
2 shallots, finely chopped
3 tbsp chopped mixed herbs, such as sage, thyme, and flat-leaf parsley
7oz sausage meat
pinch of freshly grated nutmeg
5½oz prunes (preferably Agen), finely chopped
1 tbsp duck fat
sea salt and black pepper
4 slices thick-cut bacon, cut in half widthwise

69

Bittersweet flavors complement the exquisite flavor of quail and will make you beg for more!
< SERVES 4 >

POMEGRANATE MARINATED QUAIL, GRILLED RADICCHIO, AND BITTER LEAF SALAD

4 boneless quail
sea salt and black pepper

FOR THE MARINADE
2 garlic cloves, crushed
pinch of ground cumin
2 tbsp olive oil
4 tbsp pomegranate molasses

FOR THE BITTER LEAF SALAD
1 small radicchio
dash of olive oil
dash of balsamic vinegar
1 red chicory
1 white chicory
8 mint leaves, shredded

FOR THE POMEGRANATE
DRESSING
1 garlic clove, crushed
pinch of ground cinnamon
2 tbsp pomegranate molasses
5 tbsp extra virgin olive oil
1 tbsp honey

Warm Chickpea Purée
(recipe #104)

Prepare the marinade by mixing all the ingredients together. Add the quail and toss, then marinate for 1 hour or refrigerate overnight.

Preheat a grill pan over medium heat. Cut the radicchio in half, then quarters, drizzle with olive oil, season with sea salt, and place on the hot grill pan. Cook until charred on each side, remove, and immediately drizzle with the balsamic vinegar. Leave to cool, then cut away the core and shred finely lengthwise.

To make the dressing, mix all of the ingredients with 2 tablespoons water and store at room temperature.

Preheat a grill pan, remove the quail from the marinade, and season with sea salt and pepper. Place the quail in the pan skin-side down and cook over medium heat for 3–4 minutes on either side. Remove from the heat and leave to rest in a warm place.

For the salad, halve the red and white chicory and thinly slice diagonally. Mix together with the shredded radicchio and the mint. Season, dress, and divide between four plates. Spoon a pile of chickpea purée onto each plate and top with the salad. Cut the quails in half and rest one half on top of each salad. Drizzle with the cooking juices and serve immediately.

70

As a kid I remember my mom's Sunday get-togethers laden with cakes, sandwiches, and sardines on toast too. Here's my adult version. Sometimes the most simple things in life taste the best! < SERVES 4 >

SARDINES AND CHERRY TOMATOES ON TOAST

Quarter the tomatoes and place in a bowl with the basil leaves, garlic, Parmesan, olive oil, and salt. Toss until combined, then set aside.

Drizzle the bread with a little olive oil and cook on a preheated grill pan until lightly charred on both sides.

Rub the sardines with a little more oil, season, and cook for 1–2 minutes per side (skin side first) or until cooked through.

Place an even layer of tomatoes on each piece of toast, top with a sardine (skin-side up), drizzle with olive oil, and serve immediately.

1lb 2oz cherry vine tomatoes
1 small bunch basil, leaves torn
1 garlic clove, crushed
¼ cup freshly grated Parmesan
6 tbsp extra virgin olive oil, plus more for drizzling
sea salt
4 slices ciabatta or sourdough
4 large sardines, butterflied

SMOKED MACKEREL, ASPARAGUS, AND NOODLE SALAD WITH GINGER MISO DRESSING

FOR THE GINGER MISO DRESSING

1½oz fresh ginger, peeled and finely grated

1 garlic clove, finely grated

¼ cup rice vinegar

1 tbsp soy sauce

½ tbsp superfine sugar

¼ cup sesame oil

2 tbsp yellow or red miso paste

1 bunch asparagus, woody ends snapped off

1 package soba or buckwheat noodles

dash of olive oil

sea salt and black pepper

4 smoked mackerel fillets, flaked

1 bunch cilantro, leaves picked

4 scallions, thinly sliced diagonally

1 avocado, cut into rough ¾in chunks

1 cup podded soy beans, defrosted

2 tbsp black or white sesame seeds, toasted

1 bunch watercress, picked

To make the dressing, whisk all of the ingredients together in a small bowl with 2 tablespoons water and refrigerate until required.

Bring a large pan of salted water to a boil, add the asparagus, and cook for 2 minutes. Remove the asparagus and plunge into cold water. Keep the water boiling for the noodles and cook according to the instructions on the package. Drain and place in a large bowl and toss with enough ginger miso dressing to coat.

Preheat a grill pan, toss the cooked asparagus with olive oil, sea salt, and pepper, and cook over medium heat until lightly charred; remove and leave to cool before cutting each spear into three pieces diagonally.

Toss the remaining ingredients together with the noodles and asparagus and serve immediately.

I had the great fortune of meeting Anissa Helou, who taught me the art of Moroccan cooking. Chermoula provides a wonderful fresh taste to contrast with the oily richness of mackerel. < SERVES 4 >

MARINATED MACKEREL WITH CHERMOULA AND CARROT AND OLIVE COUSCOUS

4 whole mackerel (6oz each), gutted, heads on or off
2 garlic cloves
1 tsp ground ginger
1 tsp ground cinnamon
pinch of saffron
4 tsp fennel seeds
1 red chile, finely chopped
2 tbsp olive oil

FOR THE COUSCOUS
¾ cup couscous
4 tbsp butter
2oz green olives
zest of 1 lemon, finely grated
4 tbsp cilantro, finely chopped
pinch of cumin
1 tbsp sumac
1 red chile, finely chopped
¼ cup chickpeas from a can, drained
½ cup carrots, grated

FOR THE CHERMOULA
2 garlic cloves
pinch of crushed red pepper flakes
2 tsp ground cumin
1 tsp paprika
2 tbsp lemon juice
2oz cilantro, chopped
pinch of sea salt
¼ cup light olive oil

Preheat the oven to 350°F.

Make three diagonal incisions along both sides of the mackerel.

To make the mackerel filling, pound the garlic, ginger, cinnamon, saffron, fennel seeds, and red chile with the olive oil in a mortar and pestle and use the mixture to fill the incisions in the fish. Brush the mackerel with a little olive oil, place on a hot grill pan and sear for 2 minutes on each side. Place in the oven and cook for about 5 minutes or until the mackerel is cooked through.

Next, place the couscous in a bowl, add the butter and ½ cup boiling water, cover with plastic wrap, and leave to steam for 4 minutes. Fluff with a fork, add the remaining ingredients, and season to taste.

To make the chermoula, place the garlic, spices, lemon juice, cilantro, and salt in a blender and slowly add the olive oil, blending until smooth.

Serve the mackerel with the couscous and drizzle with chermoula.

After a fabulous day out fishing for mackerel with my great friend Stephanie, we got home to find some jalapeño jelly, a bowl of new potatoes, and a bunch of mint in the fridge. And so the dish was born! < SERVES 4 >

MACKEREL WITH JALAPENO JELLY, PINE NUTS, AND MINT

Boil the new potatoes in salted water until tender. Drain and leave to cool slightly before cutting into ¼in slices. Toss with half the butter and keep warm.

Season the mackerel fillets on both sides with a little salt and pepper and brush with the oil. Place in the pan and cook over medium heat, skin-side down, for 1–2 minutes until the skin is crisp and golden (press on the fillets lightly if they start to curl upward to get a crisp effect all over).

Turn each fillet over, spoon over the jalapeño jelly, and cook for another minute. If your pan isn't large enough to do all the fillets at the same time, keep the cooked ones warm on a plate.

Serve the mackerel skin-side up. Spoon over the cooking juices and sprinkle with the pine nuts. Serve with warm buttered potatoes and a baby leaf salad.

10½oz new potatoes

3 tbsp unsalted butter

2 ultra-fresh mackerel, filleted and pin boned

sea salt and black pepper

1 tbsp olive oil

3 tbsp jalapeňo jelly mixed with a handful of finely chopped mint or Cranberry Chilli Jelly (recipe #168)

2½ tbsp pine nuts, toasted

baby leaf salad, to serve

79

An oldie, but a goldie! This recipe dates back to my Delfina days, and is inspired by Dicky, my sous chef there. A classic flavor combination, delicately brought together on a plate. < SERVES 4 >

HERB AND PINK PEPPERCORN SALMON WITH PEA SAUCE AND SUMMER VEGETABLES

Preheat the oven to 350°F.

Season the flesh side of the salmon fillets.

To make the crust, process all the ingredients in a small blender until they come together. Smear evenly over the salmon fillets and refrigerate until required. If you want to make the crust in advance, place the mixture between two sheets of parchment paper and roll out (keeps refrigerated for up to three days or in the freezer for two weeks), then cut to the size of the fish and lay on top.

To make the pea sauce, melt the butter in a pan over low heat and cook the shallots until softened. Deglaze the pan with the white wine and reduce. Add half the peas, the chicken stock, cream, salt, and sugar and cook until the peas are tender. Meanwhile, heat a non-stick ovenproof pan on the stovetop with a dash of olive oil, then add the salmon skin-side down (crust-side up) and cook for 2 minutes until crisp. Remove from the heat, then place in the oven and cook for 4 minutes, depending on the size of the fish (I like to serve my salmon a little underdone in the middle).

Bring a large pan of salted water to the boil and cook the potatoes, asparagus and fava beans, then strain. Put the remaining peas into a blender and add the hot pea sauce. Process until smooth (this helps to keep the bright green color). Pass through a fine sieve into a small pan, season with sea salt, and keep warm while the salmon is cooking.

To serve, divide the hot, buttered vegetables between four deep plates, pour over the pea sauce, and lay the salmon on top, garnished with pea shoots.

4 salmon fillets, about 6oz each

sea salt and black pepper

9oz new potatoes

4–8 asparagus spears

2/3 cup fava beans, fresh or frozen

2 tbsp butter

pea shoots, to garnish

FOR THE CRUST

2oz mint leaves, finely chopped

2 tsp crushed pink peppercorns

1 garlic clove, finely chopped

7 tbsp softened butter

1 cup fresh bread crumbs

1/3 cup flat-leaf parsley, finely chopped

2 tsp sea salt

FOR THE PEA SAUCE

4 tbsp unsalted butter

2 shallots, finely chopped

1/3 cup dry white wine

1lb 2oz frozen petit pois

1¼ cups chicken stock

2/3 cup heavy cream

pinch of sea salt

pinch of sugar

mellow sweet corn would also complement the bass and are in season the same time as porcini

porcini also go really well – blend with sea salt to make a seasoning

make into cream of corn

keep it in the family – add texture with sweet corn + porcini

pep up with spicy watercress

YUMMY!

serve RAW as carpaccio

steam

bake

bbq

stuff

82

with tangy beets + acidic blood oranges to complement the fresh sweet sea bass

perfect for a delicate light lunch

whole with fennel – or loads of herbs

#37

Star anise, orange, and vinegar bring the earthy beets to life; a few orange segments and slivers of raw sea bass add color and freshness—what a revelation. I love discovering new flavor combinations! < SERVES 4 >

BEET AND SEA BASS CARPACCIO WITH ORANGES

2 oranges, segmented, juice reserved (use blood oranges if they are in season)

⅓ cup red wine vinegar (I like Cabernet Sauvignon vinegar)

2 tbsp superfine sugar

2 star anise

2 beets, peeled and thinly sliced on a Japanese mandolin

2 tbsp extra virgin olive oil

10½oz super-fresh wild sea bass fillets, thinly sliced

sea salt and black pepper

pea shoots, sorrel, micro cress, or mint, finely torn

Heat the orange juice, vinegar, sugar, and star anise in a pan. Stir over low heat until the sugar has dissolved. Place the beets in a non-reactive shallow dish and pour in the liquid. Leave to cool, then refrigerate overnight to marinate.

To serve, arrange the beet slices overlapping on a plate. Take 2 tablespoons of marinating liquid, whisk with the olive oil, and spoon over the beets. Scatter with oranges and sliced sea bass, then season with sea salt and pepper. Sprinkle with pea shoots, sorrel, micro cress, or mint, and serve immediately.

VARIATIONS

- Omit the fish to turn into a vegetarian option—serve with spoonfuls of goat cheese instead along with some crusty bread.

Raw cauliflower couscous combined with preserved lemon, mint, and pistachio provides a perfect accompaniment to slightly sweet sea bream. A health-conscious dish packed to the "bream" with flavor. < SERVES 4 >

PAN-FRIED SEA BREAM WITH CAULIFLOWER, PISTACHIO, AND MINT COUSCOUS AND CAULIFLOWER PURÉE

To make the couscous, put the pistachios in a food processor, pulse to a bread crumb-like texture, then pour into a large bowl. Place half the cauliflower florets in the food processor and blend to a couscous-like texture. Add to the pistachios and repeat with the remaining florets. Combine with the remaining ingredients, season with sea salt, and add more olive oil and lemon juice to taste. Refrigerate for at least 1 hour before serving, to allow the flavors to infuse.

To make the cauliflower purée, place the cauliflower and milk in a small saucepan with the salt. Bring to a boil, simmer, and cook until the cauliflower is very tender, then drain, setting aside the milk. Place in a blender, add the butter and lemon juice, and process until smooth, adding a little of the reserved milk if it is too thick. Season as necessary and keep warm while you cook the fish.

Heat the olive oil in a large non-stick pan (or 2 medium pans), season the fish, and pan-fry skin-side down for 2 minutes or until crisp and golden. Flip the fish over and continue to cook for another 2–3 minutes, depending on the size of the fish.

To assemble, place a spoonful of the cauliflower purée on each plate, top with cauliflower couscous, and place a bream fillet, skin-side up, next to it. Garnish with pea shoots and a drizzle of extra virgin olive oil.

VARIATIONS

- Try adding some soaked golden raisins or chopped medjool dates and a pinch of cumin to the couscous recipe.

FOR THE "COUSCOUS"
a handful of pistachio nuts, peeled and blanched
½ cauliflower, cut into florets
juice of 1–2 lemons
4 tbsp olive oil
1 bunch mint, finely chopped
1 preserved lemon, cut into quarters, flesh removed, washed, and finely chopped
sea salt

FOR THE CAULIFLOWER PURÉE
½ cauliflower, cut into small florets
1 cup milk
pinch of sea salt
2 tbsp butter
1 tbsp lemon juice

dash of olive oil
4 sea bream fillets (also known as dorade or orata), skin scored
pea shoots, to garnish

To me, cream of corn and porcinis are a seasonal match made in heaven! I've broken this recipe down into several components; you can make one or all of them—it's up to you how far you want to take the recipe. < SERVES 4 >

SEA BASS WITH CREAMED CORN AND PORCINI POPCORN

FOR THE PORCINI POPCORN
2 tbsp olive oil
1¾oz unpopped popcorn
2 tbsp unsalted butter, softened
Porcini Salt (recipe #107)

FOR THE CREAMED CORN
3 ears sweet corn
4 tbsp unsalted butter
3-4 large shallots, finely chopped
1 garlic clove, finely chopped
1 chicken bouillon cube
1⅔ cups heavy cream
sea salt and black pepper

FOR THE PORCINIS
¼ cup extra virgin olive oil
1lb 2oz porcini or mixed wild mushrooms, wiped clean and finely sliced
sea salt and black pepper
1 garlic clove, finely chopped

FOR THE SEA BASS
4 sea bass fillets (weighing 4½-5½oz each)
dash of olive oil
2 tbsp butter
watercress sprigs

Start with the porcini popcorn. Heat the oil in a large saucepan with a tight-fitting lid. Add the kernels and cover immediately—they will begin to "pop." Cook over medium heat, moving the pan continuously until the popping stops—this will take about 2–3 minutes. Remove the pan from the heat and leave covered for a minute or else the popcorn will go flying!

Carefully remove the lid and add the butter and porcini salt to taste, setting aside some of the flavored salt for the sea bass. Toss well to mix. The popcorn can be made ahead of time and stored in an airtight container.

Next, for the creamed corn, remove the corn kernels from the cobs using a sharp knife. Heat the butter in a saucepan and gently cook the shallots and garlic until softened, but not browned. Add the corn and crumble in the bouillon cube. Stir in the cream and reduce the heat to a simmer, stirring occasionally until the corn is tender—about 25 minutes. Use a hand blender (or potato masher) to blend the mix until semi-smooth, then season with black pepper and salt, if necessary. Keep warm.

For the porcinis, heat the olive oil in a large frying pan. (Cook in batches if you don't have a large pan, otherwise you'll lower the temperature and end up stewing the mushrooms, and that would be sacrilege!) Add the mushrooms and cook over high heat for 3 minutes. Season with salt and black pepper. Add the garlic and cook for another 2 minutes, or until the mushrooms are tender. Set aside in a warm place.

Using a sharp knife, score the skin of the sea bass; this will prevent the fish from curling while cooking. Season the flesh side with the porcini salt.

Heat the olive oil in a non-stick frying pan and cook the sea bass skin-side down for 2–3 minutes until the skin is crisp and golden. Turn over, add the butter, and cook for 2–3 minutes more, or until the fish is cooked through.

To assemble, divide the creamed corn between four plates and top with some watercress sprigs and the porcinis. Place the sea bass on top, skin-side up, and sprinkle the popcorn over the top. Serve immediately.

This recipe takes strawberries right out of their comfort zone. Their sweetness balanced with ginger's gentle spice, acidic subtle rice vinegar, and salty fish sauce, combined with aromatic herbs, produce a taste sensation. < SERVES 4 >

FRIED LEMON SOLE WITH THAI-SPICED STRAWBERRY SAUCE

Heat 2 tablespoons of the oil in a pan and gently cook the chile, ginger, shallot, and garlic until soft.

In a food processor, purée the strawberries with ½ cup water and the vinegar until smooth. Deglaze the shallots with whiskey, if using. Once reduced, add the palm sugar and strawberry purée. Simmer until thickened, then add the lime juice and fish sauce.

Meanwhile, cook the fish. Heat the oil in two large frying pans and mix the cornstarch with sea salt, pepper, and the Chinese five spice. Coat each lemon sole with seasoned cornstarch and cook, flesh-side down, until golden. Carefully turn the fish over and continue to cook for another 3 minutes (depending on their size, they should take about 6–8 minutes to cook).

To serve, place each fish on a large plate, spoon over the strawberry sauce, top with the scallions and herbs, and serve with a side dish of steamed jasmine rice.

⅔ cup grapeseed oil for frying, plus 2 tbsp for the sauce

1 red chile, seeded and finely chopped

1oz fresh ginger, peeled and cut into fine strips

1 shallot, finely chopped

1 garlic clove, finely chopped

½lb strawberries, hulled and quartered

¼ cup rice vinegar

3 tbsp whiskey (optional)

2 tbsp palm sugar

juice of 1 lime

2 tbsp fish sauce

¾ cup cornstarch

sea salt and black pepper

4 tsp Chinese five spice (optional)

2 large whole lemon soles, head and top black skin removed (ask your fishmonger to do this)

2 scallions, finely chopped diagonally

1 small bunch cilantro, leaves picked

12 leaves Thai basil or Vietnamese mint

jasmine rice, to serve

#41

I had the most delicious halibut tagine while traveling in Morocco—this is my interpretation of it. You can use any skinless, meaty white fish fillets to replace the halibut if you like. A perfect dish for entertaining. < SERVES 4 >

HALIBUT, ORANGE, AND OLIVE TAGINE

pinch of saffron

1¼ cups hot fish stock or water

2 tbsp olive oil

1 onion, halved and finely sliced

2 garlic cloves, finely chopped

2 tsp ground cumin

½ tsp paprika

pinch of ground ginger

1 x 14oz can tomatoes, crushed

½ red chile, seeded and finely chopped

1 cinnamon stick

1 tbsp honey

zest and juice of 1 orange

1 small fennel bulb, quartered, cored, and thinly sliced

4 halibut steaks or 1lb 2oz skinless halibut fillets, cut into about 2oz pieces

sea salt and black pepper

2 tbsp pitted olives

¾oz cilantro, chopped

½oz flat-leaf parsley, chopped

Mix the saffron into the fish stock and leave to infuse.

Heat the olive oil in a large saucepan and gently cook the onion until soft. Add the garlic and spices and cook for 2 minutes. Add the tomatoes, chile, cinnamon, honey, orange zest and juice, and saffron-infused stock. Bring to a boil and simmer for 15 minutes before adding the fennel, then cook for another 10 minutes.

Season the fish and add to sauce; simmer for 10 minutes or until the fish is cooked. If using halibut steaks, test to see if cooked by moving the bone a little; if there is no resistance, the fish is cooked. If using fillets, the fish will need to cook for about 6 minutes. Stir in the olives and herbs and season to taste.

Serve in deep bowls with couscous or boiled potatoes.

VARIATIONS

- You can vary the fish used—monkfish would make a great alternative, as would red mullet.
- Try adjusting the flavorings a little—substitute lemons for oranges, coriander seeds for ginger, and add fennel seeds if you don't have any fresh fennel.

bring together with crunchy apple, fragrant cilantro, a little lime, and a hint of chile

combine with oyster juices and turn into a salt jelly

delicious with aromatic beer

tentacles, beaks + eyes!

ink is used to color pasta + polenta

SQUID

the world's longest vertebrate

golden rule = cook it low, cook it slow, cook it high, cook it quick

go beyond deep-fried

serve grilled with earthy lentils

marinate with fragrant acidic clementines and a touch of chile

stuff it

chile + Asian flavors - and my favorite ingredient, watermelon

OYSTERS

clean, fresh + sea salty

SEAFOOD

mussels

prawns

clams

CRAB

claws, brown meat, white meat

sweet + meaty, delicate + fresh

pair with vanilla, asparagus + crème fraiche

add to a watermelon curry - gorgeous with a splash of lime + salty fish sauce - liven up with fresh cilantro + a hint of chile

use to freshen up cauliflower soup, add lemongrass to lighten and top with crab meat

93

Most clams are bought "purged," meaning their grit has been removed; it's always best to ask, though, before buying. If they haven't been purged, you'll need to rinse and soak them in plenty of cold water. < SERVES 4 >

#42

BAKED CLAMS WITH ROSEMARY, WHITE BEANS, AND TOMATOES

Preheat the oven to 400°F.

Rinse the clams in cold water and shake dry.

Lay a large double layer of foil or parchment paper on the counter—it should be big enough to fold over the filling.

Place the clams, garlic, pepper flakes, tomatoes, beans, and rosemary on one half of the foil. Drizzle with olive oil and pour in the wine.

Fold the foil or paper over the clams, sealing the edges together to make a neat but loose parcel, making sure you allow enough room for the clams to open up.

Transfer the parcel to a roasting pan and bake in the oven for 10–12 minutes, until the clams are open. Carefully open up the parcels and serve as they are, with crusty bread.

1lb 12oz clams
2 garlic cloves, finely sliced
pinch of crushed red pepper flakes (optional)
12 cherry vine tomatoes, halved
¾ cup cooked cannellini beans, rinsed
sprig of rosemary, leaves stripped
extra virgin olive oil, for drizzling
½ cup dry white wine
bread, to serve

VARIATIONS

- This is another recipe for you to take on a culinary journey! For an Asian twist, add aromatics such as ginger, lemongrass, chiles, and cilantro and omit the rosemary.
- Try cooking these clams on the grill.
- You could try using mussels instead of clams.

The delicate flavor of lemongrass matched with cauliflower combine beautifully to create a soup with finesse; top with sweet crabmeat to add a touch of decadence. < SERVES 4 >

CAULIFLOWER AND LEMONGRASS SOUP WITH CRAB

2 tbsp unsalted butter

3-4 large shallots, finely chopped

4 sticks lemongrass, tough outer leaves removed and set aside

2 tbsp ginger, finely chopped

1 cauliflower (about 1½lb), outer leaves removed

2⅓ cups milk

⅔ cup heavy cream

sea salt and black pepper

2-2½oz picked white crabmeat

micro cilantro leaves or lemon balm, to serve

Heat the butter in a large saucepan, add the shallots, and cook over low heat until softened.

Finely chop the lemongrass and add to the shallots with the ginger. Tie the reserved tough outer edges together with an elastic band.

Core the cauliflower and break into florets, then finely slice and add to the pan. Add the milk and tied lemongrass and bring to a boil, stirring constantly. Reduce the heat to a simmer and cook until the cauliflower is tender (about 15 minutes).

Add the cream, reheat a little, then remove the tied lemongrass. Blend the soup in batches until smooth (pass through a fine sieve if not smooth enough). Season with sea salt and pepper.

Pour into shallow warmed soup bowls. Top with the crabmeat and a few micro cilantro leaves, or some finely chopped lemon balm.

VARIATIONS

- The soup can also be made with scallops instead of crabmeat, if you prefer. Season 8 scallops with a little sea salt and pepper. Add a dash of olive oil to a hot pan, place the scallops in flat-side down, and cook over medium-high heat until seared and golden. Flip over and cook for another minute on the other side (no more). Serve as above.

I can still remember the taste of the most amazing paella I've ever eaten. It was several years ago, in a little shack on Sóller beach in Majorca. My version uses quinoa, a nutty and protein-filled grain. < SERVES 4 GENEROUSLY>

SEAFOOD AND QUINOA PAELLA

Combine the stock and saffron in a pan over low heat and bring to a simmer. Remove from the heat and leave for 5 minutes to allow the saffron to infuse.

Heat the oil in a large paella or frying pan over medium heat. Add the chicken thighs and brown on each side. Move the chicken to the side of the pan and add the onion, red pepper, and garlic and cook, stirring, for 5 minutes or until the onion has softened.

Add the paprika and tomatoes and cook for 3 minutes, stirring. Add the quinoa, season with salt and pepper, and pour over the saffron-infused stock, bringing it to a boil. Reduce the heat to low and cook uncovered for 15 minutes or until quinoa is almost tender.

Add the beans and cook for 3 minutes. Add the mussels and shrimp, pushing lightly into the quinoa, then sprinkle in the peas. Cover loosely with foil and cook for about 8 minutes or until the shrimp have changed color and the mussels have opened. Turn off the heat and leave to rest for 5 minutes.

Discard any unopened mussels and serve straight from the pan, sprinkled with parsley and with the lemon wedges on the side.

1 quart chicken stock

large pinch of saffron

2 tbsp olive oil

4 chicken thighs, skin on and bone in

1 small onion, finely chopped

1 red bell pepper, seeded and finely chopped

2 garlic cloves, finely chopped

1 tsp smoked paprika

3 vine-ripe tomatoes, peeled and finely chopped

1¾ cups quinoa

sea salt and black pepper

⅔ cup green beans, trimmed and halved

14oz mussels, debearded

12 jumbo shrimp, shells and heads on

⅓ cup frozen peas, defrosted

large handful of flat-leaf parsley, coarsely chopped

lemon wedges, to serve

One of my favorite ways to eat squid. It's fresh, flavored without the usual deep-fried preparation—perfect for a summer barbecue. I'm salivating as I write! < SERVES 4 >

CLEMENTINE AND CHILE GRILLED SQUID

FOR THE MARINADE
4 red chiles
finely grated zest of
2 clementines
4 tbsp olive oil

**FOR THE SMOKED CHILE
AND CLEMENTINE DRESSING**
juice of 6 clementines
¼ cup olive oil
dash of Chardonnay vinegar
(if unavailable, use white
wine vinegar)

8 medium-large squid tubes
(calamari)
½ cauliflower, cut into florets
1 cup milk
sea salt and black pepper
2 tbsp butter
sea salt and black pepper
micro cilantro, to serve

First, make the marinade. Pierce the chiles with the tip of a knife and cook on a hot grill pan until the skins are blackened. Remove from the pan, leave to cool, then peel away the charred skins. Cut in half lengthwise, scrape away the seeds, and discard. Finely chop the chiles, setting aside half for the dressing. Mix the clementine zest with the remaining charred chiles and olive oil. Set aside while you prepare the squid.

Remove the wings and outer skin of the squid. Using a knife, make a split lengthwise along one side of each squid to open up the tube. Scrape out and discard any guts and cartilage. Lightly score incisions in a criss-cross fashion (at about ¼in intervals). Place the squid tubes in the marinade, mix well, and marinate for at least 30 minutes or overnight.

To make the dressing, heat the clementine juice and reduce by half or until it's syrupy. Remove from the heat and whisk with the chiles set aside earlier, olive oil, and vinegar. Season with a pinch of sea salt. This dressing will keep in the refrigerator for several days.

Next, make a cauliflower purée. Set aside three florets and cut the remaining ones into small even-sized pieces. Place in a saucepan with the milk and a pinch of sea salt. Cook over low heat until the cauliflower is tender. Drain the cauliflower, setting aside the milk; liquefy the cauliflower until smooth, adding the butter, seasoning, and enough of the milk set aside earlier to make a nice, smooth consistency. Keep warm.

Thinly slice the reserved florets lengthwise on a mandolin. (They need to be wafer thin, so mind your fingers.)

Remove the squid from the marinade, season with sea salt, and cook on a preheated grill pan, scored-side down. As the squid cooks, it will slowly roll into a tube. Turn the squid over after about 3–4 minutes and cook on the other side.

Serve the squid on cauliflower purée, drizzle with clementine chile dressing, and sprinkle with shaved cauliflower and micro cilantro.

Juicy peaches, brimming with flavor and refreshing Thai herbs, shrimp and chile–a quintessential summer lunch in itself. If you don't have rice paper rolls, just toss in a bowl with dressing and serve as a salad. < MAKES 16 ROLLS >

#46

SHRIMP, PEACH, AND THAI BASIL VIETNAMESE RICE PAPER ROLLS

Cook the rice noodles according to the instructions on the package. Drain and rinse thoroughly with cold water so they don't stick together, then set aside to cool.

Fill a large, shallow bowl with warm water. Dip one rice paper into the water to soften (this will take 10–40 seconds, depending on how thick they are). Remove and lay on a damp kitchen towel. Arrange three shrimp down the center with some herbs, noodles, peanuts, peach, and lettuce. Don't overfill or it will be too fat and impossible to roll.

Fold the edge of the paper closest to you over the filling, fold in the sides, then roll up tightly to make a neat parcel. Set aside on a plate while you repeat with the remaining rice papers and fillings. Cover the rice paper rolls with a damp kitchen towel until you are ready to eat.

To make the dipping sauce, place the chile, garlic, and palm sugar in a mortar and grind to a smooth paste. Stir in the remaining ingredients, alog with 1 tablespoon of water.

Serve the sauce in little dipping dishes with the rice paper rolls.

VARIATIONS

- The shredded smoked paprika chicken from recipe #6 makes a great alternative to shrimp.

2oz rice vermicelli noodles
16 round rice papers
48 large cooked peeled shrimp
½ small bunch mint, leaves picked
small bunch cilantro, leaves picked
32 leaves Thai basil or Vietnamese mint
⅓ cup unsalted roasted peanuts, coarsely chopped
1 peach, halved, thinly sliced, then julienned
1 baby gem lettuce, halved, finely shredded, lengthwise

FOR THE DIPPING SAUCE
1 small bird's-eye chile, seeded and finely chopped
2 small garlic cloves
1 tbsp palm sugar
juice of 2 limes
4 tbsp fish sauce
1 tbsp rice wine vinegar

Sea salty fresh oysters paired with subtle bitter and delicate aromatic beer—here are two flavors that really love one another. I've added a zesty fresh and crisp salad to complement them. **< SERVES 4 >**

OYSTERS WITH BEER JELLY, GREEN APPLE, AND LIME AND CILANTRO SALAD

12 oysters

¾ cup Belgian beer (I like to use Duvel)

3 sheets gelatin, soaked in cold water

FOR THE APPLE SALAD

1 Granny Smith apple

zest of 1 lime and juice of ½ lime

micro cilantro, or 2 tbsp finely chopped cilantro, to garnish

1 tsp finely chopped green chiles, seeds removed

dash of extra virgin olive oil

crushed ice, to serve

Open the oysters using an oyster knife and strain the liquid through a sieve into a saucepan. Remove the oysters from their shells and refrigerate. Rinse the bottom shells and set aside for serving.

To make the jelly, add the beer to the oyster liquid in the pan and bring to a simmer over medium heat. Remove from the heat.

Squeeze the soaked gelatin sheets to remove any excess water and stir into the hot beer mixture until completely dissolved. Pour through a fine sieve into a shallow plastic container. Leave to cool, then refrigerate for about 2 hours or until set.

To make the salad, thinly slice the apple, preferably on a Japanese mandolin if you have one, and cut into fine strips. Combine the apple with the lime zest and juice, cilantro, and chiles and dress with a dash of extra virgin olive oil.

To serve, cut the jelly into fine dice and divide between the 12 oyster shells you set aside. Place an oyster on top of each and garnish with salad. Serve the oysters on crushed ice.

VARIATIONS

- Use agar agar to set the beer as opposed to gelatin.

You may have gathered by now that I have an obsession with watermelon which, in the case of this recipe, makes a delicate, refreshing curry; one of my most talked about recipes—perfect for a balmy summer's evening. < SERVES 4 >

48

WATERMELON AND SEAFOOD CURRY

To make the curry, liquefy 3½lb of the watermelon in a blender or food processor until smooth. Cut the remaining watermelon into ½in cubes and set aside.

Heat half of the oil in a large frying pan. When hot, gently cook the onion, ginger, and garlic until soft. Add the chile, lemongrass, and spices and cook for another minute. Add the liquified watermelon, bring to a boil, then simmer until reduced by half. This should take about 20–30 minutes.

To prepare the seafood, heat the remaining oil in a large frying pan. Season the squid with salt and pepper and cook in two batches over high heat for 3 minutes per batch. Set aside.

Once the curry has reduced, add the squid, crabmeat, cilantro, and the diced watermelon that you set aside and gently heat through. Add fish sauce and lime juice to taste—the curry should be hot, sweet, and sour. Serve immediately.

4½lb watermelon (the seedless variety works best), rind and seeds removed

2 tbsp grapeseed oil

1 onion, finely chopped

2 tbsp fresh ginger, finely chopped

1 garlic clove, finely chopped

1 red chile, seeded and finely chopped

1 lemongrass stick, finely chopped

1 tsp turmeric

2 tsp ground coriander

1 tsp cumin seeds

pinch of cayenne pepper

1lb 2oz cleaned squid, sliced into rings

sea salt and black pepper

3½oz meat from crab claws

1 bunch cilantro, finely chopped

dash of fish sauce, to taste

juice of 1–1½ limes, to taste

add tomatoes, garlic + herbs to create your own baked beans

absorb flavor like a sponge

finish with herbs; cherry tomatoes + feta – fab or sourdough toast or with lamb

cook in orange or apple juice for extra flavor

high in protein + contains all the amino acids needed for good health

comfort

use in sweet or savory dishes

QUINOA

cook for breakfast – just like oatmeal!

is an ancient food native to South America

pronounced "keen-wah"!

Italians eat lentils on New Year's Eve – they symbolize money + good fortune for the coming year

Italy

Greece

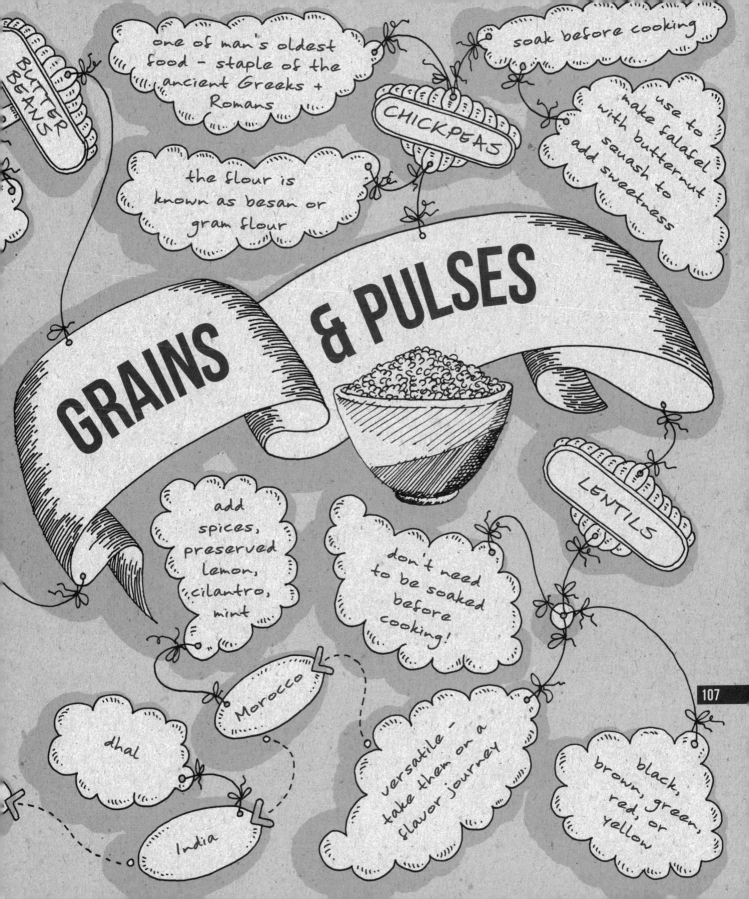

BUTTER BEANS

one of man's oldest food - staple of the ancient Greeks + Romans

soak before cooking

CHICKPEAS

use to make falafel with butternut squash to add sweetness

the flour is known as besan or gram flour

GRAINS & PULSES

add spices, preserved lemon, cilantro, mint

don't need to be soaked before cooking!

LENTILS

Morocco

dhal

India

versatile - take them on a flavor journey

black, brown, green, red, or yellow

Pretty much a pantry soup. I had to put together a last-minute appetizer one day—and this soup was the result! Fabulous for summer. < SERVES 4 >

CHILLED WHITE BEAN AND GREEK BASIL SOUP WITH SHRIMP, LEMON, AND CHILE

2 tbsp olive oil

3 shallots, peeled and thinly sliced

2 garlic cloves, finely chopped

2 x 14oz cans cannellini beans

1½ cups light chicken stock

handful of Greek basil, coarsely chopped

sea salt and black pepper

pinch of chili powder

juice of 1 lemon

FOR THE SHRIMP TOPPING

2 tbsp olive oil

16 raw tiger shrimp, peeled

sea salt and black pepper

pinch of crushed red pepper flakes

1 lemon, segmented and chopped

1 tbsp Greek basil leaves

Heat the olive oil in a saucepan, add the shallots and garlic, and cook over low heat until softened (about 10 minutes). Add the beans and chicken stock, bring to a boil, then reduce the heat to a simmer and cook for about 10 minutes.

Leave to cool a little before blending in batches, adding the basil to each batch, until smooth. Season with sea salt and pepper, and add a pinch of chili powder and lemon juice to taste. If the soup seems too thick, add a little water. Leave to cool and refrigerate, covered, until required.

To make the shrimp topping, heat the oil in a frying pan and season the shrimp with sea salt, pepper, and pepper flakes. Cook the shrimp for 2 minutes until translucent. Transfer to a bowl and toss with lemon and basil leaves.

Top the chilled soup with the shrimp mixture and drizzle with olive oil. Serve immediately.

VARIATIONS

- Sorrel would make a great substitute for the Greek basil; you will need about 10 leaves, deveined, for the soup.
- Tangerine flavored olive oil is gorgeous drizzled on top of the soup instead of regular olive oil.

I think these beans are best made the day before so the flavors have time to infuse. I use dried beans for this recipe because they absorb all the delicious flavors of the cooking liquid. < SERVES 4–6 >

50

GREEK BEANS ON TOAST WITH FETA AND TOMATOES

Soak the beans overnight in plenty of cold water.

The next day, drain and rinse the beans and place them in a large saucepan. Cover with plenty of cold water and bring to a boil. Reduce the heat and simmer until just tender (about 50 minutes).

Preheat the oven to 300°F.

Drain the beans, setting aside both the cooking liquid and the beans.

Heat the olive oil in an ovenproof pan. Add the onion and garlic and cook until softened over medium heat. Add the tomato paste and cook for another minute. Add the plum tomatoes, sugar, reserved beans, and 2⅓ cups of the liquid set aside earlier. Season with salt and pepper, cover with foil or a lid, and cook for a further hour. Remove the cover, then stir and cook for another 30 minutes until most of the liquid has been absorbed and the beans are tender.

Season to taste, then stir in the herbs and cherry tomatoes (if using) and serve warm on toasted sourdough sprinkled with feta and drizzled with olive oil.

1lb 2oz dried butter beans
½ cup olive oil
1 onion, finely chopped
3 garlic cloves, finely chopped
1 tbsp tomato paste
2¼lb vine plum tomatoes, peeled and coarsely chopped
1 tsp sugar
sea salt and black pepper
¼ cup parsley, finely chopped
3 tbsp oregano, finely chopped or 3 tsp dried
3½oz cherry tomatoes, halved (optional, but I like the contrast of cooked and fresh tomatoes)
1⅓ cups feta cheese, crumbled
toasted sourdough, to serve
olive oil, for drizzling

#51

When I first tasted quinoa I thought the health benefits outweighed the taste. I decided this needed to change and experimented cooking it in flavored stocks and fruit juices. Here's the result of one experiment. < SERVES 4 >

ORANGE AND SUMAC SCENTED QUINOA

2 tbsp olive oil

1 carrot, finely chopped

1 celery rib, finely chopped

1 small onion, finely chopped

¾ cup quinoa

finely grated zest of 1 orange

¾ cup freshly squeezed orange juice

sea salt and black pepper

1oz toasted almond flakes

½ bunch cilantro, finely chopped

½ bunch mint, finely chopped

1 avocado, diced into ½in cubes

2 tsp sumac, plus a pinch for garnish

shiso sprouts, if available

Heat the oil in a medium pan. Add the carrot, celery, and onion and cook over medium heat until tender. Add the quinoa and cook for 1 minute while stirring.

Add the orange zest, juice and 3½ tablespoons water and bring to a boil. Reduce to a simmer, cover and cook for 15 minutes until the quinoa is tender and the orange juice has been absorbed. Season with sea salt and pepper.

Leave to cool a little before stirring through the almonds, cilantro, mint, avocado, and sumac. Garnish with shiso sprouts if available and sprinkle with a pinch of sumac.

VARIATIONS

- I like to serve this with oily fish, such as mackerel.
- It's also delicious served chilled with shrimp or on its own.
- Great with chile-roasted feta too.
- Try cooking the quinoa in apple juice instead of orange juice.

#52

I'm constantly being told to eat more protein to maximize the benefits of working out. Whether you exercise or not though, here's your very own 15-minute protein fix. And it's quick and easy to make, too. < SERVES 4 >

MOROCCAN-SPICED LENTILS WITH PAN-FRIED SALMON AND AVOCADO CREAM

FOR THE LENTILS

1 tbsp light olive oil

1 onion, finely chopped

2 garlic cloves, finely chopped

1 tbsp grated fresh ginger

2 tsp cumin

1 tsp cinnamon

2 tsp paprika

1 tsp ground coriander

¾ cup pre-cooked brown or puy lentils

⅓ cup chicken stock or boiling water

small bunch cilantro

½ small bunch mint

juice of ½ lemon

4 salmon fillets, skin on

sea salt

1 tbsp grapeseed or olive oil

⅛ cup raisins, presoaked in hot water to plump (optional)

1 preserved lemon, quartered, flesh removed, rinsed, and finely chopped (optional)

1 tbsp chopped green/red chile (optional)

FOR THE AVOCADO CREAM

1 ripe avocado

juice of 1 lime

dash of milk

Heat the oil in a medium saucepan. Add the onion and cook over medium heat until softened. Add the garlic, ginger, and spices and cook for another 2 minutes.

Meanwhile, cook the salmon. Season the salmon flesh with salt. Heat a large non-stick pan over medium heat, add a little oil, and, when hot, carefully place the salmon skin-side down in the pan.

Add the lentils to the saucepan with the spicy onion mix and add the stock. Cook over low heat for about 5 minutes.

Now make the avocado cream. Halve the avocado, remove the pit, and scoop out the flesh. If you've got a hand blender, process all the ingredients in a pitcher with a pinch of salt and purée until smooth. You want a yogurt-like consistency (add a little extra milk, if necessary). If you don't own a hand blender, mash the avocado with a fork or potato masher or pass through a sieve, then mix with the lime juice and milk and season with salt.

Turn the salmon fillets over—the skin should be crispy by now.

Finely chop the herbs and add to the lentils. Season to taste and finish with a squeeze of lemon juice. Add raisins, preserved lemon, and chile, if you'd like.

Serve the lentils topped with salmon and a spoonful of avocado cream.

VARIATIONS

- Serve with roasted butternut squash, grilled zucchini with lemon and mint, or purple sprouting broccoli with pine nuts and tahini yogurt.
- These lentils are great served cold the next day with some flaked smoked mackerel or crumbled feta, or even just on their own with a little Greek yogurt.

114

Earthy puy lentils jazzed up with citrus and spice-a perfect partner for Ginger Beer and Tangerine Glazed Ham (recipe #12). If you have any leftovers, try serving with some pan-fried shredded squid. < SERVES 4–6 >

#53

CHILE AND TANGERINE BRAISED LENTILS

Heat the olive oil in a large saucepan over medium heat. Add the carrot, onion, celery, garlic, and chile and cook until the vegetables begin to soften (about 5 minutes).

Meanwhile, place the lentils in a fine-mesh colander and rinse well under cold water. Drain before adding to the vegetables.

Add the hot stock and about two thirds of the tangerine juice. Bring to a boil, then reduce the heat and simmer for 20–25 minutes or until the lentils are al dente and most of the liquid has been absorbed. Add a little more stock if the lentils look a little dry during cooking.

Remove from the heat and stir in the tangerine zest and remaining juice. Season, then leave to cool a little before stirring through the crème fraîche and parsley. Serve warm or at room temperature.

2 tbsp olive oil
1 carrot, finely chopped
1 onion, finely chopped
1 celery rib, finely chopped
1 garlic clove, finely chopped
1 red chile, seeded and finely chopped
1 cup puy lentils
1¾ cups chicken or vegetable stock, heated
zest of 2 tangerines and juice of 6 tangerines
sea salt and black pepper
2 tbsp crème fraîche
small bunch flat-leaf parsley, finely chopped

VARIATIONS

- If serving with Ginger Beer and Tangerine Glazed Ham (recipe #12), use the hot ham cooking liquid to cook the lentils instead of chicken or vegetable stock.
- Finish with chopped fresh mint or cilantro. Or vary the recipe by replacing the lentils with fresh borlotti beans—you'll need to cook for an additional 30–40 minutes, so will need a little extra stock or water.
- Lentils are one of the most versatile ingredients, so try taking them on a flavor journey, from Morocco to the Mediterranean: omit the ginger and spices, add a dash of tomato paste, some fennel seeds (optional), cherry tomato halves, and continue to cook as above. Finish with lots of fresh basil and parsley, a squeeze of lemon, and some extra virgin olive oil. Stir through a spoon of ricotta the next day, or serve topped with a little grated Parmesan.

115

My autumnal version of falafel—sweet and lightly fragranced with fresh cilantro. The salad adds freshness and color. Great as a snack or light lunch.

< MAKES ABOUT 24 >

BUTTERNUT SQUASH FALAFEL

Preheat the oven to 400°F.

Cut the butternut squash into ¾–1¼in chunks. Place in a roasting pan and drizzle with the olive oil, season with sea salt, and cook for about 20 minutes or until tender. Leave to cool.

When cool, place the butternut squash pieces in a food processor, together with any juices. Add all the remaining ingredients, except the flour, and process to a coarse paste. Season to taste. Transfer to a bowl and add enough flour to make a smooth mix. Refrigerate for up to 1 hour to firm the mixture up.

The mixture should be sticky rather than really wet, so add a little more gram flour if necessary. Wet your hands and form into balls about ¾–1¼in in diameter. Roll in the remaining gram flour, place on a sheet lined with floured parchment paper, and refrigerate until required.

Heat the oil to 325°F and fry the balls in batches for 3–4 minutes until golden. Remove from the oil and drain on paper towels.

For the salad, wash and shave the fennel using a mandolin or sharp knife. Drizzle over the pomegranate molasses, and scatter and toss with the pomegranate seeds, scallions, parsley and salad leaves. Season with salt and pepper.

Serve the falafel with the salad, tahini yogurt sauce, and pita bread on the side so your guests can build their own sandwiches.

1½lb butternut squash, peeled and seeded
2 tbsp olive oil
sea salt
2 garlic cloves, finely chopped
2 tsp ground cumin
½ tsp ground coriander
pinch of cayenne pepper
½ tsp baking powder
1 x 14oz can chickpeas, rinsed and drained
1¼ cups cilantro, finely chopped
1 tbsp lemon juice
1 cup gram (chickpea) flour, plus ½ cup for dusting
vegetable or peanut oil, for frying

FOR THE FENNEL, PARSLEY, AND POMEGRANATE SALAD
1 fennel bulb
2 tbsp pomegranate molasses
seeds of 1 pomegranate
2 scallions, finely sliced
⅓ cup flat-leaf parsley, leaves picked
2 handfuls of mixed salad leaves, such as mizuna and baby red chard
sea salt and black pepper

Tahini Yogurt Sauce
(recipe #103)
pita bread, to serve

Ooooh, roasted sweet butternut squash, earthy lentils, fresh mint, sour salty feta, mint, and sticky caramelized spiced onions—what more could you ask for? Delightful! < SERVES 4 >

ROASTED BUTTERNUT SQUASH FILLED WITH CARAMELIZED PUY LENTILS AND FETA

2 small butternut squash, about 1¼lb each

4 tbsp olive oil

sea salt and black pepper

¾ cup puy lentils

2 onions, halved and thinly sliced

2 garlic cloves, finely chopped

2 tsp cumin seeds

2 tsp ground cumin

1 tsp ground cinnamon

½ tsp sweet paprika

pinch of cayenne pepper

⅔ cup feta cheese, crumbled

¼ cup pine nuts

2 tbsp chopped mint

1 tbsp chopped flat-leaf parsley

juice of 1 lemon

seeds from ½ pomegranate, to garnish

Heat the oven to 400°F.

Wash the butternut squash and carefully cut them in half lengthwise. Using a spoon, scoop out the seeds and fibrous center and discard. Put the squash halves on a baking sheet cut-side up, drizzle with 1 tablespoon olive oil, season, and roast in the oven for about 35 minutes or until the flesh is tender. Remove from the oven and leave to cool slightly.

While the squash is cooking, simmer the lentils for about 30 minutes, until al dente, and drain.

When the squash is cool enough to handle, scoop out some flesh, leaving a border of ½in, then coarsely chop the flesh and put it in a bowl.

Heat 3 tablespoons olive oil in a large frying pan, add the onions and garlic, and cook until beginning to caramelize (about 15 minutes). Add the spices and cook for 2 minutes more. Add the lentils, squash flesh, and ⅔ cup hot water and simmer for 8 minutes, until most of the water has been absorbed. Remove from the heat and stir through the feta cheese, pine nuts, herbs, and lemon juice. Season to taste with salt and pepper.

Spoon the mixture equally between squash halves and cook in the oven for 10–15 minutes. Serve garnished with pomegranate seeds.

VARIATIONS

- You could use 1 cup precooked lentils, or cook the lentils ahead of time. As another time saver, the filling can be prepared in advance.

118

what about a savory carrot baklava?

add sour feta, crunchy almonds, fresh chopped dill + sweet chewy dates

great together!

use fresh and add grated carrots, fresh mint, and chopped red chile to make a refreshing salad

Middle Eastern adventure

great in a spiced carrot purée

top with dukkah

cinnamon

earthy pungent cumin

cardamom

anise

sweet + woody

cilantro

complement with spice

ginger

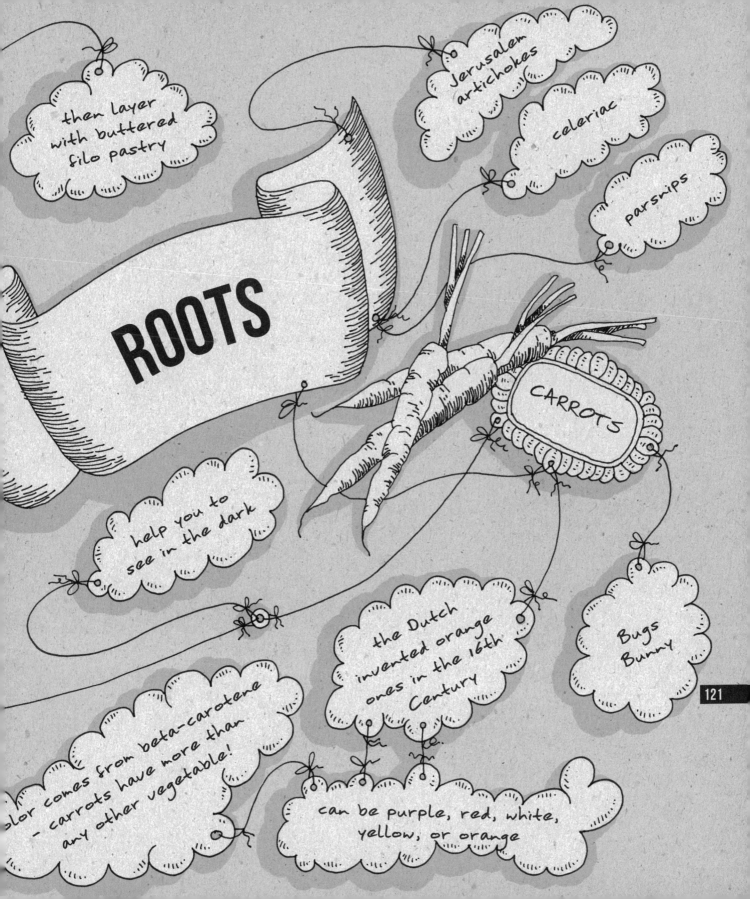

then layer with buttered filo pastry

Jerusalem artichokes

celeriac

parsnips

ROOTS

CARROTS

help you to see in the dark

the Dutch invented orange ones in the 16th Century

Bugs Bunny

olor comes from beta-carotene - carrots have more than any other vegetable!

can be purple, red, white, yellow, or orange

I experimented combining mozzarella and Porcini Salt and it was a complete revelation. This flatbread recipe was designed to showcase their harmonious relationship.

< SERVES 4 GENEROUSLY>

56

NEW POTATO FLATBREAD
WITH ARUGULA, MOZZARELLA, AND PORCINI SALT

In a small bowl, combine the yeast, sugar, and water and leave in a warm place until foaming (about 10 minutes).

Combine the flour and salt in a mixing bowl and pour in the olive oil and yeast mix. If you have a food processor with a dough hook attachment, use this to form a dough; otherwise, get mixing by hand until the dough is cohesive. Turn onto a lightly floured surface and knead until smooth and elastic (about 10 minutes). The dough will be quite sticky at first, but it'll come together once you start kneading—rubbing a little olive oil into your hands will make this easier.

Place the dough in a clean, oiled bowl, cover, and leave in a warm place until doubled in size (about 1–1½ hours).

Preheat the oven as high as it will go.

Cook the potatoes in salted water until just tender. Drain, leave to cool, then cut into ¼in slices. Place a large upturned baking sheet in the oven.

Turn out the dough and punch down. On a lightly floured surface, roll and gently stretch the dough into a rounded rectangle to fit the baking sheet. Place on a piece of parchment paper, drizzle with olive oil, and lightly season with Porcini Salt and pepper. Top with mozzarella and potato slices, then season again with Porcini Salt and pepper. Carefully slide onto the hot upside-down baking sheet and bake in the middle of the oven until the base is crisp (about 10–12 minutes).

Remove the flatbread from the oven, top with the arugula, then drizzle lightly with olive oil and serve.

VARIATIONS

- These flatbreads are really good with a poached egg on top.

FOR THE FLATBREAD
½oz active dried yeast
¾ tbsp sugar
¾ cup warm water
3⅓ cups all-purpose flour
2 tsp sea salt
1 tbsp extra virgin olive oil, plus extra for drizzling (or use truffle oil)

FOR THE TOPPING
7oz new potatoes, washed
3 tbsp olive oil, plus extra for drizzling
Porcini Salt (recipe #107)
freshly ground black pepper
9oz ball of buffalo mozzarella
handful of arugula

#57

The earthy Jerusalem artichokes and spicy sweet chorizo complement each other beautifully. Deep undertones also run through from the chestnuts, and the caramelized apples add a bit of "zing." A luxurious soup. < SERVES 4 >

JERUSALEM ARTICHOKE AND CHESTNUT SOUP WITH CHORIZO AND APPLE

4 tbsp unsalted butter

4 shallots, thinly sliced

2 garlic cloves, thinly sliced

2 tbsp chopped thyme leaves

2¼lb Jerusalem artichokes, peeled, sliced, and placed in acidulated water

3 tbsp sherry

2oz cooked chestnuts (I use the vacuum packed ones)

1 quart chicken stock

sea salt and black pepper

½ Macintosh apple, peeled, cored, and cut into ½in dice

1 tbsp superfine sugar

2 tbsp of butter

olive oil

1 cooking chorizo

⅔ cup cream (optional)

2 tbsp chopped flat-leaf parsley, to serve

Heat the butter in a large pan. Add the shallots and cook over low heat for 10 minutes until softened and slightly caramelized. Add the garlic, thyme, and Jerusalem artichokes and cook for another 5 minutes. Add the sherry, chestnuts, and chicken stock and bring to a boil. Reduce to a simmer, season with salt and pepper, and cook until the artichokes are tender (about 15–20 minutes).

Meanwhile, preheat a frying pan, toss the apple in the sugar, and pour into the hot pan. The sugar will start to caramelize as it hits the pan; add the 2 tbsp butter and cook for 1 minute over high heat until golden. Set aside.

Wipe the pan with paper towels and preheat again. Slice the chorizo and cook in the hot frying pan with a little olive oil for 3 minutes and set aside.

Process the artichoke mixture in a blender until smooth, then return to the pan, adding cream if desired. Check the seasoning and warm through. Add a little extra stock or water if it's too thick.

Divide the soup between four bowls. Top with the chorizo, drizzle with chorizo oil, and scatter with apple and a sprinkling of parsley. Serve with crusty bread.

I love food like this! I normally make my dukkah with hazelnuts, but I think the almonds provide a better combination with the carrot purée.

< SERVES 8 >

SPICED CARROT PURÉE WITH DUKKAH

FOR THE DUKKAH
⅓ cup almonds, blanched (skinless)
⅓ cup coriander seeds
1½ tbsp cumin seeds
1½ tbsp sesame seeds
sea salt and black pepper

FOR THE CARROT PURÉE
2¼lb carrots, cut into ¾in pieces
⅓ cup extra virgin olive oil, plus more for drizzling
2 tbsp lemon juice
1 tbsp harissa
1 tsp ground cinnamon
pinch of ground ginger
sea salt and black pepper

To make the dukkah, toast the almonds in a medium pan over medium heat until golden. Transfer to a work surface to cool a little, then finely chop. Transfer to a bowl.

Add the coriander and cumin seeds to the pan and toast until fragrant (about 2 minutes). Transfer to a mortar and pestle, leave to cool completely, then coarsely grind and mix with the almonds.

Toast the sesame seeds until golden, leave to cool, then grind, together with 1 teaspoon sea salt. Add to the almond mixture and season with black pepper.

To make the carrot purée, cook the carrots in a large saucepan with water until tender. Drain and return the carrots to pan over medium heat to dry thoroughly (about 1 minute). Remove from the heat and mash the carrots with a potato masher or process until smooth in a blender.

Gradually, blend in the olive oil, lemon juice, harissa, cinnamon, and ginger. Season with sea salt and pepper.

Transfer the carrot purée to a large, flat bowl. Using the back of a spoon, smooth the surface, raising a little at the edges, drizzle with olive oil, and sprinkle with the dukkah. Serve at room temperature with hot Turkish or pita bread or a flatbread.

VARIATIONS

- Substitute the carrots for butternut squash or use a green pumpkin; roast in the oven until tender, then follow recipe above.
- For flavor variations, add some chopped dried apricots to the carrot purée or blend with some cooked red lentils. Finish with chopped cilantro or mint for a fresher, less earthy flavor.

126

A simple summer salad that, served with *Carrot Baklava* (recipe #63), lends additional texture along with color. Alternatively, you could serve it with *Pomegranate Labneh* (recipe #105). < SERVES 4 AS AN ACCOMPANIMENT >

#59

CARROT AND HERB SALAD

Lightly peel the carrots, cut off the roots, and trim the carrot tops to ½in in length. Place in a pot of cold salted water and bring to a boil. Simmer until just tender (about 6 minutes). Drain and cut in half lengthwise.

Whisk together the vinegar, oil, and honey and pour over the hot carrots. Season with salt and pepper, toss with the herbs, and serve immediately.

VARIATIONS

- To make this salad go further, serve with Orange and Sumac Scented Quinoa (recipe #51) or with Middle Eastern Kebab (recipe #5).
- Additional extras to add to the salad: flaked almonds, chile-roasted feta, spiced sunflower seeds, and cooked barley.

8 baby carrots (if you can get a variety of colors, so much the better)

a few carrot leaf tops

2 tsp Chardonnay vinegar (if unavailable, use white wine vinegar)

1 tbsp extra virgin olive oil

1 tbsp honey

sea salt and black pepper

½ bunch purslane, if available (if not, use baby spinach)

few sprigs flat-leaf parsley, picked

By cooking the parsnips in various ways you will not only create different tastes, but textures that will complement each other beautifully. This is a perfect salad to serve as an appetizer or as a light lunch. < SERVES 4 >

TRUFFLED PARSNIP SALAD

First, peel, core, and dice the parsnips into ½in cubes. Heat a large, non-stick frying pan and add the butter. Once hot, add the parsnips, season with sea salt and pepper, and cook over low heat, stirring occasionally, until golden, caramelized, and tender. Don't rush this stage—the parsnips need to caramelize slowly to achieve the perfect flavor. Use as big a frying pan as possible, so the parsnips cook in one even layer.

Once caramelized and tender, remove the parsnips from the heat and drizzle with the truffle oil. Gently crush about one third with a potato masher or a fork and season as necessary.

For the thyme-roasted parsnips, preheat the oven to 400°F. Peel the parsnips and cut in half lengthwise. Cut each half in half again or into thirds, depending on the size of the parsnips, and cut out the woody cores. Place in a roasting pan, drizzle with olive oil, season with sea salt and pepper, and sprinkle with the thyme. Roast in the oven for about 10 minutes, until golden and tender.

Now for the purée. Peel, halve, and core the parsnips and slice into ¾in pieces. Place in a saucepan, add the milk and a pinch of salt, and simmer until soft. Drain the parsnips, reserving the cooking liquid and process while hot in a blender, adding the lemon juice and olive oil until smooth but thick. Add a little of the parsnip liquid to thin, if necessary. Season if needed.

Warm the roasted parsnips and the purée; the truffled parsnips should be warm or served at room temperature. Spread a slick of purée onto each plate and top with truffled parsnips followed by the roasted ones.

Toss the watercress leaves with the vinegar and oil and place on top of the parsnips. Sprinkle with the shaved pecorino and serve immediately.

FOR THE TRUFFLED PARSNIPS
2 large parsnips
7 tbsp unsalted butter
sea salt and black pepper
4 tbsp truffle oil

FOR THE THYME-ROASTED PARSNIPS
2 large parsnips
3 tbsp olive oil
sea salt and black pepper
2 tsp thyme leaves

FOR THE PARSNIP PURÉE
2 parsnips
¾ cup milk
pinch of sea salt
1 tbsp lemon juice
1 tbsp olive oil

TO SERVE
1 bunch watercress, picked into small sprigs
2 tbsp Cabernet Sauvignon vinegar (if unavailable, use red wine vinegar)
2 tbsp truffle oil
3oz shaved hard sheep's milk cheese, such as pecorino

VARIATIONS

• Try serving the truffled parsnips with roasted chicken or pheasant.

An idea that literally popped into my head one day, adding some spark to pancakes. This is a great way of introducing fruit and vegetables to a sweet snack!

< MAKES ABOUT 24 PANCAKES >

CARROT AND APPLE PANCAKES

11 tbsp unsalted butter
3 tbsp corn syrup or honey
½ cup light muscovado sugar
½ tsp baking powder
pinch of sea salt
2 tsp ground cinnamon
1 carrot, grated
1 green apple, grated
2½ cups rolled oats

Preheat the oven to 350°F. Line a 12 x 8in baking sheet with parchment paper.

Gently melt the butter in a saucepan. Add the corn syrup, sugar, baking powder, salt, and cinnamon.

Remove from the heat and stir in the carrot, apple, and porridge oats until just combined.

Spoon the mixture onto the prepared baking sheet and smooth with the back of a spoon. Cook in the oven for 30–35 minutes until golden and fairly firm to touch.

Remove from the oven and cut pancakes while hot. Leave to cool, before transferring to a wire rack.

VARIATIONS

- Try adding ¼ cup chopped skin-on almonds for a touch of texture.
- Add the zest of 1 orange.
- Experiment with different fruit and vegetable combinations.

130

Celeriac is not one of the prettiest of vegetables, but its taste makes up for its looks! A member of the parsley family, it tastes a little like celery. You'll need to cut away the skin before using. < SERVES 4 >

CELERIAC AND BUTTER BEAN SOUP SWIRLED WITH SAGE BROWN BUTTER

Warm the butter in a large pan, add the onion, celery, and garlic, and cook until softened. Add the celeriac and cook for another 5 minutes. Add the butter beans and milk or stock and cook over low heat until the celeriac has softened (about 30–40 minutes).

Add the cream and warm through, then process in a blender until silky smooth. Add a dash of water if a little too thick.

Transfer the soup back to the pan, reheat gently, and season with sea salt and black pepper.

To make the sage brown butter, place the butter in a saucepan and heat until it begins to foam. Add the sage and cook until the butter has browned, then squeeze in the lemon juice. Spoon the sage brown butter over the soup or cool and gently reheat when ready to use.

4 tbsp unsalted butter
1 onion, finely chopped
1 celery rib, finely chopped
2 garlic cloves, finely chopped
1 medium celeriac (about 1¼lb), coarsely chopped into ¾in pieces
1 x 14oz can butter beans, drained and rinsed
2½ cups milk or chicken stock
¾ cup heavy cream
sea salt and black pepper

FOR THE SAGE BROWN BUTTER
7 tbsp butter
10 sage leaves
1 tbsp lemon juice

#63 Baklava is usually sweet, but this recipe is anything but "usual"! Roasted carrots are combined here with sour feta, crunchy almonds, and aromatic dill to create a delicious vegetarian dinner sensation. < SERVES 6–8 >

CARROT, DILL, ALMOND, AND FETA BAKLAVA

3 tbsp olive oil

1 large onion, halved and thinly sliced

1 garlic clove, finely chopped

2lb carrots, peeled, halved, and thinly sliced

1 bunch fresh dill, finely chopped, including roots (or 3 tsp dried)

3 tsp ground cinnamon

finely grated zest of 1 lemon

juice of ½ lemon

sea salt

1 package filo pastry (9 sheets)

7 tbsp butter, melted

⅔ cup whole almonds, blanched and blended to a coarse breadcrumb consistency

1⅔ cups feta cheese, crumbled

4 tbsp honey

Preheat the oven to 350°F.

Heat the olive oil in a large saucepan. Gently cook the onion over low heat until caramelized (about 15 minutes); don't rush this part—you want the onion to be nice and sticky, so use the time to prepare the other ingredients while it's cooking.

Stir in the garlic, carrots, dill, cinnamon, and lemon zest and juice and heat for another 2 minutes. Season with salt and add 3⅓ cups water. Cook over medium heat until most of the liquid has been absorbed and the carrots are tender, stirring frequently and adding more liquid if necessary. This will take about 25 minutes.

Remove from the heat and, using a hand blender, process about one third of the carrot mixture, then mix with the remaining carrots.

Unfold the filo pastry and cut in half lengthwise. Keep it covered with a damp cloth while you work to prevent it from drying out. Brush a 12 x 8in baking sheet with a little melted butter. Brush one sheet of filo with butter, top with another, brush again, and top with another. Line the baking sheet with this three-sheet layer. (Filo pastry brands differ, so cut according to your pan size.)

Spread half the carrot mixture over the pastry and sprinkle with half the almonds and feta. Sandwich another three sheets of filo together as before with melted butter and place on top of the carrot mixture. Cover with the remaining carrot mixture, almonds, and feta and a final three-sheet layer of filo.

Lightly score the top with a knife, cutting into 6–8 diagonals or squares. Brush with butter and sprinkle with a little water.

Place in the oven and bake for 30–35 minutes until golden. Remove from the oven and leave to cool a little before drizzling with honey.

The baklava is delicious with Carrot and Herb Salad (recipe #59).

133

Eggplant and halloumi are two of my favorite ingredients, the former because of their versatility and the latter because it reminds me of my childhood! Great as a side with slow-roasted lamb. < SERVES 8 >

EGGPLANT-WRAPPED HALLOUMI WITH POMEGRANATE LABNEH

Brush each eggplant slice with olive oil and season well with sea salt and pepper.

Preheat a grill pan or outdoor grill and cook the slices in batches over medium heat until golden and tender. Set aside to cool.

Place a piece of the halloumi at the end of each eggplant slice. Squeeze over the lemon juice and sprinkle with a little dried oregano.

Roll each eggplant slice up to enclose the halloumi and place on a baking sheet. Heat the parcels under a broiler or in the oven until the cheese begins to soften. Alternatively, wrap them in foil and heat on a grill.

To make the pomegranate molasses dressing, whisk all of the ingredients together with 1 tablespoon water until emulsified.

Serve the halloumi with some arugula dressed with pomegranate dressing. Scatter with pomegranate seeds and serve with the labneh on the side.

VARIATIONS

- I like to serve this dish scattered with a few crushed blanched almonds to add a little texture.
- If you can't find pomegranate molasses, try making your own, using 2⅓ cups pomegranate juice, ⅓ cup lemon juice, and ½ cup sugar. (Use less sugar if your juice already has added sugar.) Combine all the ingredients, heat, and reduce to a simmer until thickened to a syrup.

2 eggplant, cut lengthwise in ¼-½in slices (you'll need 8 slices in all)

olive oil, for brushing

sea salt and black pepper

2 x 9oz packages of halloumi, each sliced into four lengthwise

juice of ½ lemon

large pinch of dried oregano

handful of arugula

pomegranate seeds

Pomegranate and Mint Labneh (optional)—recipe #105

FOR THE POMEGRANATE MOLASSES DRESSING

1 garlic clove, crushed

5 tbsp extra virgin olive oil

2 tbsp pomegranate molasses

dash of red wine vinegar

1 tbsp honey

sea salt and black pepper

137

This to me would be a perfect campside soup. Smoky eggplant and winter warming spices with a touch of tartness from the pomegranate molasses. A soup with depth of flavor just waiting to be cooked. < SERVES 4 >

SMOKED EGGPLANT, TOMATO, AND RED LENTIL SOUP

1 eggplant
1 tbsp olive oil
1 onion, finely chopped
2 garlic cloves, finely chopped
1½oz fresh ginger, finely chopped
1 red chile, seeded and finely chopped
2 tsp garam masala
8 vine-ripe tomatoes, peeled and finely chopped, juices reserved
¾ cup red lentils
sea salt and black pepper
4 tbsp Greek yogurt
2 tbsp pomegranate molasses
2 tsp sumac
1 tbsp coarsely chopped flat-leaf parsley

Pierce the eggplant with a fork and place directly on an open flame or on a preheated grill pan. Cook until charred all over and softened. Place in a colander and leave to cool.

Heat the oil in a large saucepan. Add the onion and cook until softened and lightly browned. Add the garlic and ginger and cook for another 2 minutes. Then add the chile and garam masala and cook for a further minute before adding the tomatoes. Reduce the heat to a simmer and cook for 10 minutes.

Meanwhile, peel the eggplant and finely chop the flesh. Place in a colander to drain off the bitter juices.

Rinse the red lentils in a fine sieve until the water runs clear, then add to the tomatoes. Add 1⅔ cups hot water and the eggplant flesh and cook over low heat until the lentils are tender (about 20 minutes), stirring frequently.

Purée two thirds of the soup in batches. If the soup is a little too thick, add a dash of hot water. Season with sea salt and pepper.

Ladle the soup into bowls and top with a swirl of yogurt, pomegranate molasses, and a sprinkling of sumac and parsley. Serve hot.

Charred, smoky eggplant blended with tahini, garlic, and lemon juice make a dip bursting with flavor. Perfect as an accompaniment to Middle Eastern Kebab (recipe #5) or Eggplant-Wrapped Halloumi (#64). < SERVES 4 >

BABA GHANOUSH

Prick the eggplant all over with a fork; this will stop them from bursting. Place the eggplant directly over a gas flame or on a barbecue grill and cook until the skin is blackened and the flesh soft, turning frequently. (If you have an electric stove, you can place under a hot broiler instead—unfortunately, you won't end up with such a smoky flavor though.)

Place the eggplant in a colander until cool enough to handle. Holding onto the stem, peel away and discard the blackened skins. Place the eggplant flesh in a colander to drain off the bitter juices.

Place the eggplant flesh in a blender and pulse to break up. Add the tahini (best to stir it in the jar before using), garlic, cumin, sea salt, and a little lemon juice. Pulse to mix, retaining a little texture. Add more lemon juice and extra salt if required. (If you prefer a smoother texture, process until smooth and slowly blend in the olive oil while the motor is running.)

Serve with warm pita bread for dipping.

2 large eggplant
3 heaping tbsp tahini
2 garlic cloves, finely chopped
pinch of ground cumin
sea salt
juice of 1 lemon
⅓ cup olive oil

EGGPLANT

#67

I promise you, cooking the eggplant to a dark brown color really does make all the difference. Thank you Neil and Angela at Rockpool in Sydney, Australia for the inspiration for this recipe. < SERVES 4 AS A SIDE DISH>

EGGPLANT MULL

1 cup olive oil

1 large eggplant, cut in half lengthwise, then into ¼in slices

2 garlic cloves, finely chopped

pinch of cayenne pepper

1 tsp paprika

½ tsp ground cumin

4 plum vine tomatoes, peeled and cut into quarters

sea salt

juice of ½ lemon

¼ bunch cilantro, picked

¼ bunch flat-leaf parsley, picked

Heat two thirds of the oil in a large frying pan, add half the eggplant slices, and cook until well browned. Remove and drain on paper towels. Repeat with the remaining eggplant.

Heat the remaining oil gently, add the garlic, and swirl around the pan off the heat to infuse. Add the spices and tomatoes and return to low heat. Cook for 5 minutes to soften the tomatoes before adding the eggplant. Cook over low heat for another 5 minutes. Season with sea salt.

Remove from the heat, add the lemon juice, and leave to cool to room temperature before stirring in the cilantro and parsley.

VARIATIONS

- Serve with fish or meat or by itself with flatbread and labneh or Tahini Yogurt Sauce (recipe #103).
- Try adding some chopped preserved lemons or some chopped dates for extra sweetness.

140

add some goat cheese

natural affinity with vanilla - slightly peppery

or serve raw shaved into wafer-thin slices

tender and bursting with flavor - stronger than green beans

my favorite green bean!

ITALIAN FLAT BEANS

grow on wigwams - beautiful red flowers

complement with a little chile, add some acidity with sweet cherry tomatoes, and season with salty anchovies

mix with bread crumbs + Parmesan too - roll into kaftades and fry

OR

toss through pasta

toss together with spaghetti + top with Parmesan for a speedy dinner. Yummy!

ASPARAGUS

GREENS

Zucchini

young shoots of the cultivated lily plant

a delicacy

were a luxury in Ancient Egypt, Greece + Rome

packed with vitamins A + C

has more potassium than a banana

same family as melon, cucumber + squash

has an affinity with lemon - feta too

add some mint, dill + parsley

make into fritters with Parmesan for a tasty treat

blanch, fry, roast, grill, or boil

Don't let the title put you off—"Zucchini Fritters" just didn't do the recipe justice. This is a vegetarian version of a Greek classic usually made with lamb. Perfect for a picnic or light lunch. < SERVES 4—6 >

ZUCCHINI KEFTEDES

Blanch the zucchini in boiling water for 2 minutes then drain and squeeze dry in a cloth.

Heat a little oil in a pan and cook the onions until soft. Place in a bowl and combine with the zucchini, cheeses, herbs, eggs, and half the bread crumbs. Season with salt and pepper. If the mixture is too wet, add a few more bread crumbs. Chill in the fridge for about 1 hour to allow the mix to set.

Taste for seasoning before shaping into walnut-sized balls. Season the flour with salt and coat the balls in flour.

Heat a little oil and fry the balls in batches until golden on all sides (about 2–3 minutes). Remove and drain on paper towels.

Serve with a squeeze of lemon and tzatziki .

1lb zucchini, trimmed and grated
vegetable oil, for frying
2 tbsp grated onion
1 cup feta cheese, crumbled
¾ cup grated Parmesan
2 tbsp chopped parsley
2 tbsp chopped mint
2 eggs, beaten
6–8 tbsp fresh bread crumbs
sea salt and black pepper
all-purpose flour, for dusting
1 lemon, to serve
tzatziki, to serve

VARIATIONS

- Serve with Spiced Carrot Purée (recipe #58) or with grilled halloumi. Also delicious with Dill and Lemon Marinated Lamb (recipe #18) or pan-fried fish, shrimp, or squid.

#69

Spinach, raisin, and pine nuts have a natural affinity to one another. Use as an accompaniment to fish or lamb, and take your spinach to new heights by adjusting the recipe using the variations below. < SERVES 4 AS A SIDE DISH >

SPINACH WITH GARLIC, RAISINS, AND PINE NUTS

2 tbsp olive oil

1lb 2oz spinach, stems removed

2 garlic cloves, finely chopped

2 tbsp pine nuts, lightly roasted

2 tbsp raisins, soaked in hot water for 15 minutes and drained

sea salt

Gently heat half the olive oil in a large frying pan, add the spinach, and cook until it starts to wilt. Remove from the heat and drain the spinach in a colander.

Return the pan to the heat, add the remaining olive oil, then cook the garlic until softened, but not browned. Add the spinach, pine nuts, and raisins. Season with sea salt and cook for another minute.

VARIATIONS

- Add some diced potatoes to the spinach to make a more substantial side dish.
- Try adding some capers—they pair deliciously with raisins.
- Soak the raisins in sherry vinegar to create a little punch. You could also add a some chopped red chile to the garlic.

146

Another recipe oozing with Greek flavors—lemon and dill add punch to the fava beans. Best made the day before—and it is well worth the effort to double pod the beans. < SERVES 4 AS A SIDE DISH >

LEMON AND DILL BRAISED FAVA BEANS

Shell the fava beans and remove their outer coats. If using fresh, the easiest way to do this is to blanch them for 1 minute in boiling water, then refresh in cold water. If using frozen, defrost in water, then pop the beans out of their shells.

Heat the oil in a large pan and gently cook the onion until softened without color. Add the garlic, sugar, and sea salt, and cook for another 2 minutes. Add the fava beans and stock and simmer over low heat for about 20 minutes until the beans are tender and most of the liquid has evaporated.

Remove from the heat, stir in the lemon juice and dill, and season to taste. Let stand for 1 hour before serving or, preferably, overnight.

Serve at room temperature, sprinkled with a little feta, if desired.

2¼lb fresh fava beans in their shells (or 13oz frozen)

¼ cup extra virgin olive oil

1 onion, finely chopped

1 garlic clove, finely chopped

pinch of sugar

pinch of sea salt

1 cup chicken stock or water

juice of 1 lemon

small bunch dill, finely chopped

feta cheese, to serve (optional)

VARIATION

- Try adding 2 globe artichokes to the ingredients above—you will need to prepare these ahead of time. Place the artichokes in a large pot of acidulated water with a pinch of salt. Cover with paper and weigh down with a plate or small lid. Cook for about 20 minutes until tender and the tough outer leaves can be easily removed (the timing will depend on the size of the artichokes). Remove all the tough outer leaves and trim the stems, cut in half, remove the fuzzy choke, and cut each half into thirds. Place in acidulated water until required, to prevent discoloration. Add the artichokes to the recipe when cooking the onion, then continue as above, adding a little extra stock if required.

147

#71

Fantastic, tangy sorrel leaves, bursting with flavor, are often available from farmers' markets, along with dandelion leaves. Sorrel has a natural affinity with eggs and oily fish. < SERVES 4 >

ROAST TENDERSTEM BROCCOLI SALAD WITH SOFT-BOILED EGG AND SORREL DRESSING

1¾lb tenderstem broccoli, trimmed to florets of equal size

3 tbsp olive oil

sea salt and black pepper

4 eggs, at room temperature

1½oz pecorino or Parmesan cheese, freshly shaved

1 head dandelion leaves, washed and cut into 2in lengths

2 handfuls of mixed baby leaves, such as ruby chard, baby spinach, mizuna, and mustard

FOR THE DRESSING

2½ tbsp shallots, finely chopped

¼ tsp garlic, finely chopped

¼ cup extra virgin olive oil

¼ cup olive oil

3 tbsp Chardonnay vinegar (if unavailable, use white wine vinegar)

½ tbsp wholegrain mustard

3 sorrel leaves, finely chopped

Preheat the oven to 375°F.

Place the broccoli in a bowl, drizzle with olive oil, season with salt and pepper, and toss well. Scatter into a roasting pan and roast in the oven for 3–5 minutes or until the broccoli is tender. Remove from the oven and leave to cool.

Place the eggs in boiling water and cook for 4–5 minutes (depending on how soft you like the yolks), then remove from the pan, plunge into cold water, and peel carefully.

Next, make the dressing. Whisk all of the ingredients together and refrigerate until required.

Place the broccoli, cheese, and leaves in a large bowl, toss with dressing to coat, gently season, and serve, garnished with torn soft-boiled eggs.

VARIATIONS

- This recipe would be equally delicious made with cauliflower in place of the broccoli.
- Substitute the soft-boiled hen's eggs for duck's eggs if you can get them; allow a little longer for cooking though.
- If sorrel is unavailable, substitute with parsley, dill, tarragon, or chervil.

148

The asparagus season doesn't last too long, so I always try to embrace this wonderful unique flavor when the opportunity is there. Best to start the oil a day ahead to allow the flavor to infuse. < SERVES 4 >

SHAVED ASPARAGUS, GOAT'S CURD, AND VANILLA CROSTINI

FOR THE VANILLA OIL
1 vanilla bean
½ cup light olive oil

FOR THE GOAT'S CURD
5½oz goat cheese
3 tbsp crème fraîche

8 large asparagus spears
sea salt
2 tbsp lemon juice
1 tbsp chopped chervil
(optional)

FOR THE CROSTINI
4 slices crusty bread (I like to use ciabatta)
olive oil, for drizzling

To make the oil, halve the vanilla beans lengthwise and scrape out the seeds, mixing all but a pinch with the oil. Add the beans and leave to infuse at room temperature, covered, for a minimum of 1 day.

To make the curd, trim away any rind from the cheese and cut into small pieces. Place in a blender and add the reserved vanilla seeds. Pulse to break down before adding the crème fraîche. Pulse again until smooth, being careful not to overblend causing the curd to split. (If you don't have a blender, use a potato masher to break the cheese down.) If preparing ahead, chill in the refrigerator and remove 20 minutes before serving.

Using a mandolin set over a large bowl (or a vegetable peeler), shave the asparagus lengthwise into wafer-thin strips. Season with sea salt and add the lemon juice and chervil, if using. Stir the vanilla oil well and pour half of it over the asparagus; toss and set aside while preparing the crostini.

Preheat a grill pan. Drizzle the bread slices with olive oil, place on the hot grill pan, and cook until crisp and golden.

Remove the crostini from the heat, spread the curd over the bread, and top with the shaved asparagus. Drizzle with the remaining vanilla oil and serve.

VARIATIONS

- To simplify the recipe, top the crostini with a young goat cheese and omit the curd altogether (you will need 4½oz in total).
- Omit the goat cheese and blend a little white crabmeat with a spoonful of crème fraîche or mayonnaise, season, mix with chopped chervil, and serve with the crostini and shaved asparagus.

I love the process of making gnocchi, and green olives add a new dimension. Fresh seasonal greens including asparagus and peas add an abundance of flavor to an otherwise everyday Italian staple. < SERVES 4 >

GREEN OLIVE GNOCCHI WITH WILTED GREENS

Preheat the oven to 400°F.

To make the gnocchi, place the potatoes on a non-stick baking sheet and cook until tender, about 1–1½ hours. While still hot, halve and scoop out the flesh, then pass through a fine sieve, potato ricer, or mouli into a bowl.

Transfer the potatoes to a clean work surface dusted with flour. Mix with the olives, sea salt, pepper, and nutmeg. Make a well in the center, pour in the egg, and gradually work in two thirds of the flour. Bring the mixture together with your hands to form a smooth, soft dough, adding more flour if necessary.

I always like to test a little of the dough by cooking a small piece in boiling salted water. Cook until the gnocchi floats; if it falls apart, add a little more flour. Check for seasoning and adjust as necessary.

Cut the dough into four, then roll each piece into a sausage ½in thick. Cut each sausage into ¾in pieces and place on a baking sheet lined with parchment paper and sprinkled lightly with flour. You can make the gnocchi ahead of time and refrigerate until required.

Bring a large saucepan of salted water to a boil. Cook the gnocchi in batches (use the parchment paper as a chute to help you transfer them to the pan) until they come to the surface (about 1–2 minutes). Count to 10, then transfer, using a slotted spoon or sieve, to a bowl of iced water. Drain, drizzle, with olive oil and set aside.

Bring a clean saucepan of salted water to a boil. Blanch the peas and asparagus until tender, remove and refresh in iced water, then drain and set aside. Add the chard leaves and blanch until tender; refresh in iced water, drain, coarsely chop, and set aside.

Heat the oil in a large non-stick frying pan over high heat. Add the butter and, once foaming, add the gnocchi. Cook until just starting to color. Add the asparagus, peas, chard leaves, and broccoli, tossing gently to combine. Add the spinach, lemon zest, and juice and cook until just wilted. Warm through, season to taste, and serve immediately, drizzled with oil and scattered with pecorino.

FOR THE GNOCCHI

2¼lb large russet potatoes

2oz pitted green olives, coarsely chopped

sea salt and black pepper

pinch of freshly grated nutmeg

1 egg, beaten

1 cup bread flour, plus extra for dusting

4½oz podded peas (that's about 11½oz unpodded, or 4½oz frozen petit pois)

1 bunch asparagus, trimmed and cut into 1¼in pieces

½ bunch Swiss chard, leaves only (about 7oz) or substitute with kale

3 tbsp of olive oil

2 tbsp unsalted butter, diced

9oz broccoli, cut into miniature florets

7oz baby spinach

finely grated zest and juice of ½ lemon

3½oz pecorino, shaved or grated

I so look forward to green bean season. What could be better than freshly picked beans, cooked and tossed in salted butter? Well, apart from this recipe, of course—a quick, easy, and very yummy dinner! < SERVES 4 >

GREEN BEAN, ANCHOVY, AND TOMATO SPAGHETTI

Heat the olive oil in a large frying pan or wok. Once hot, remove from the heat and add the garlic, pepper flakes, and anchovies. Gently swirl the pan to infuse the oil; if the oil is too hot, the garlic will burn and the sauce will taste bitter. If the oil is too hot, add some of the tomatoes—they will immediately lower the temperature.

Add the cherry tomatoes (hopefully you didn't have the oil too hot!), sea salt, and tomato paste and simmer over low heat for about 5 minutes until the tomatoes have softened.

Meanwhile, cook the spaghetti in a large pan of boiling, salted water according to the package instructions. Four minutes before the end of its cooking time, add the green beans. Before draining the pasta, add 2 tablespoons of the cooking water to the tomato sauce to loosen it a little.

Drain the pasta and quickly mix with the tomato sauce, flavor with some pepper and olive oil and a little salt if necessary.

Toss with the basil leaves and serve immediately, topped with Parmesan. Italians will be cursing me—they think it's sacrilege to serve Parmesan with fish and pasta, but I love it!

2 tbsp olive oil

2 garlic cloves, finely chopped

pinch of crushed red pepper flakes (optional)

12 salted anchovy fillets, coarsely chopped

10½oz cherry tomatoes, halved

pinch of sea salt

2 tbsp tomato paste

¾lb spaghetti

1 cup green beans, trimmed

freshly ground black pepper

olive oil

sea salt

handful of basil leaves (optional), torn

½ cup Parmesan, grated or shaved

VARIATIONS

- Replace green beans with juliennes (thin strips) of zucchini.
- Replace the anchovies with cooked crabmeat or shrimp; just toss through at the end with the pasta.
- Vegetarians can omit the anchovies and mix through with some crumbled feta and maybe a sprinkling of fresh mint leaves and a little lemon zest.
- Fold through some arugula—they add a hint of peppery spice!
- If you have any leftover roast or braised lamb, shred it and add to the tomato sauce, with or without the anchovies.

scent with aromatic fig leaves

mix goat's milk with yogurt for a panna cotta

love it sprinkled over peas with a little dill + lemon

made from ewe's + goat's milk

FETA CHEESE

feta must be produced in Greece + has legal designation. By law feta is cured for at least 3 months in brine

salty + sour

sweeten with confectioners' sugar

= a sensational summer salad – serve with bbq lamb

sweeten with pomegranate molasses

flavor with orange flower water or rosewater

mix with crunchy watermelon

toss with almonds

cow, goat, buffalo, sheep, or camel!

one cow yields about 200,000 glasses of milk per lifetime!

cream

MILK

cheese

rice pudding

mix with mascarpone to make a delicate, delicious cream

DAIRY

with a twist - chai masala

sour, thick + creamy - sweeter with honey

YOGURT

probiotics are good for you - they aid the body's intestinal flora

produced by bacterial fermentation of milk "yogurt cultures"

in 500BC yogurt + honey was the food of the Gods!

#75

I've taken chai to another level here by using it as the base for a light rice pudding. It's delicious with Earl Grey Roasted Apricots (recipe #86) or chocolate. I also love to eat this pudding cold for breakfast. < SERVES 4 >

MASALA CHAI RICE PUDDING

FOR THE CHAI
4 green cardamom pods
4 cloves
1 cinnamon stick, lightly crushed
1¼in piece of fresh ginger, sliced
4 black peppercorns
4 tbsp black tea leaves
¼ cup palm or superfine sugar
1 cup milk

FOR THE RICE PUDDING
1 cup pudding rice
2 tbsp butter, diced
2½ tbsp cornstarch
1 cup milk
¼ cup palm or superfine sugar (optional)

To make the chai, lightly crush the cardamom pods, cloves, and cinnamon with a mortar and pestle.

Put 2½ cups water in a saucepan and add the crushed spices, ginger, and black peppercorns. Bring to a boil, then reduce to a simmer for a few minutes. Remove from the heat, add the tea, and leave to infuse for 5–10 minutes.

Add the sugar and milk to the pan, return to the heat, and bring almost to a boil. Remove from the heat and leave to steep for 4–5 minutes, before straining.

To make the pudding, place the rice, chai, and butter in a medium-sized saucepan and bring to a boil. Once boiling, reduce the heat to a simmer, stir, and cover. Cook over low heat for about 25 minutes, stirring occasionally, until the rice is tender.

Mix together the cornstarch and milk to form a smooth paste. Once the rice is cooked, stir in the cornstarch mixture, bring back to a boil, and cook for another 5 minutes, stirring continuously. For a sweeter rice pudding, stir in the optional sugar of your choice until dissolved. Serve at once.

VARIATIONS

• Experiment with different flavor teas such as jasmine, Earl Grey, or ginger, for example.

156

#76

A refreshing summer salad. Serve alone for breakfast, for lunch with grilled shrimp, or for dinner with some barbecued lamb. It's best made just before serving, so the watermelon doesn't emit too many juices. < SERVES 4 >

FETA AND WATERMELON SALAD

1lb 2oz watermelon, chilled
2 tbsp pomegranate molasses
2 tbsp extra virgin olive oil
2 tsp rosewater
1⅓ cups feta cheese
small handful of mint leaves
½ cup toasted almond flakes

Cut the watermelon flesh into large cubes, removing as many seeds as possible. Place in a large bowl and drizzle with the pomegranate molasses, olive oil, and rosewater.

Coarsely dice the feta, tear the mint leaves, and add together with the almonds. Toss with the watermelon. Serve immediately.

In my "Modern Vegetarian" book I made a gorgeous cake with oranges, almonds, and semolina. I decided to replace the orange with rhubarb and see what happened. All good, and this recipe was the result! < SERVES 8 >

YOGURT, RHUBARB, AND ALMOND SYRUP CAKE

Preheat the oven to 350°F.

First roast the rhubarb. Combine the rhubarb, 2 tablespoons sugar, orange zest, and orange flower water in a baking dish, cover with foil, and roast in the oven for 10 minutes or until tender. Leave to cool and drain off the cooking juices for the syrup.

Reduce the oven temperature to 325°F. Grease and line the bottom of a 10in springform cake pan.

Cream the butter with the sugar until pale. Beat in the egg yolks one at a time, then sift in the flour, baking powder, semolina, and almonds. Add the yogurt and the roasted rhubarb, stirring gently until just combined.

Pour the mixture into the prepared pan and bake for about 1 hour until a skewer inserted into the center of the cake comes out clean. Check after 45 minutes and cover with foil, if necessary, to prevent the cake from becoming too brown.

Meanwhile, make the syrup. Put the reserved cooking juices into a pan with the honey and ⅓ cup water. Slowly bring to a boil over low heat. Reduce the heat and simmer until syrupy (about 10 minutes).

Remove the cake from the oven and pierce all over with a skewer. Pour the syrup over the warm cake and leave to cool in the pan.

Serve the cake at room temperature with some crème fraîche.

7oz rhubarb, trimmed and cut into 1½in lengths
2 tbsp superfine sugar
finely grated zest of 1 orange
2 tbsp orange flower water
12 tbsp (1½ sticks) butter
½ cup superfine sugar
3 egg yolks
¼ cup all-purpose flour
1½ tsp baking powder
1⅓ cups semolina
1 cup ground almonds
⅓ cup Greek yogurt
3 tbsp honey
crème fraîche, to serve

VARIATIONS

• This cake would be delicious served with a zingy fruit sorbet such as blood orange and pomegranate.

A quick and easy trifle-layers of soft, spiced ginger cake, sweetened with rhubarb and topped with decadent rose-scented cream. Definitely a trifle to take on a flavor journey! < SERVES 8 >

RHUBARB, ROSEWATER, AND GINGER TRIFLE

Heat 1⅓ cups water and the sugar together in a medium saucepan until the sugar has dissolved. Add the rhubarb and cook over medium heat for 5 minutes, or until the rhubarb has softened. Strain the mixture, setting aside the cooking liquid, and leave to cool. Stir the Grand Marnier into the cooking liquid, if using.

Whisk the mascarpone, Greek yogurt, rosewater, and confectioners' sugar together in a bowl until thickened. Set aside.

Place a slice of ginger cake in the bottom of each of four wine glasses or tumblers and drizzle with enough cooking liquid to moisten without drenching the sponge. Place a spoonful of the cooled rhubarb into each glass, and continue layering in this way until you have used up the cake and the rhubarb. Divide the mascarpone mixture between the glasses, sprinkling each with almonds (if using) and stem ginger, then serve.

¾ cup superfine sugar

4–6 sticks rhubarb, trimmed, peeled, and chopped into ¾in pieces

2 tbsp Grand Marnier (optional)

9oz mascarpone

⅔ cup Greek yogurt

2 tsp rosewater

⅓ cup confectioners' sugar

½ Jamaican ginger cake, sliced into 8 pieces

1-2 tbsp toasted almond flakes (optional)

2 pieces preserved stem ginger, finely chopped

VARIATIONS

- Try substituting sponge fingers or an orange and almond cake for the ginger cake.

- Use ginger wine instead of Grand Marnier.

- Add a layer of strawberry slices, marinated in a splash of rosewater and a sprinkling of sugar.

- Take your trifle to new heights by making a rose-scented rhubarb jelly. Soak 2 gelatin sheets in cold water. Place 14oz rhubarb in a saucepan with a piece of grated ginger, 1⅓ cups confectioners' sugar, and ⅓ cup water. Cover and simmer over medium heat until the rhubarb is soft enough to mash (about 10 minutes). Strain and push through a fine sieve into a bowl. Squeeze the gelatin of its water and stir into the warm rhubarb syrup until dissolved. Leave to cool, then stir in 2 tsp rosewater. When the jelly has just begun to set, pour over the second layer of rhubarb and place in the refrigerator until completely set (about 2 hours). Top with rose-scented cream, as above.

This recipe is inspired by the awesome Brett Graham—chef at The Ledbury, London. Don't be deterred by the fig leaves: If you're lucky enough to have a fig tree, or a neighbor who does, just pluck a few. < SERVES 4 >

DRIED FIG LEAF AND GOAT'S MILK PANNA COTTA

4 fig leaves, washed and dried
9½fl oz heavy cream
1½ sheets of gelatin
⅓ cup goat's milk
⅓ cup confectioners' sugar
½ cup natural yogurt
1 fresh fig, sliced
Dried Fig and Polenta Biscuits, to serve (optional—recipe #109)

Wash the fig leaves thoroughly, pat with paper towels, and leave to dry in a warm place for about 1 week. In the summer, leave them outside—they'll take no time. If you have a food processor, strip the dried leaves from their cores and blend to a powder; if not, pound with a mortar and pestle to crush a little.

Pour the cream into a saucepan. Bring to a boil over low heat, remove from the heat and add the powdered fig leaves. Cover with plastic wrap, and leave to infuse for 1 hour.

Soak the gelatin sheets in cold water.

Pour the goat's milk into a saucepan and heat to just under boiling point. Remove from the heat, squeeze the gelatin sheets of water, and add to the milk. Stir to dissolve.

Pass the fig-leaf-infused cream through a fine sieve into a large bowl and mix with the goat's milk. Discard the fig leaves.

Gently whisk the confectioners' sugar and yogurt into the cream and milk mixture and pour into coffee cups or molds. Leave to cool a little, then cover and refrigerate until set (about 3–4 hours).

When ready to serve, dip the molds briefly in hot water, run a round-edged knife around each panna cotta, gently shake, and invert onto plates.

Serve with slices of fresh figs and the biscuits.

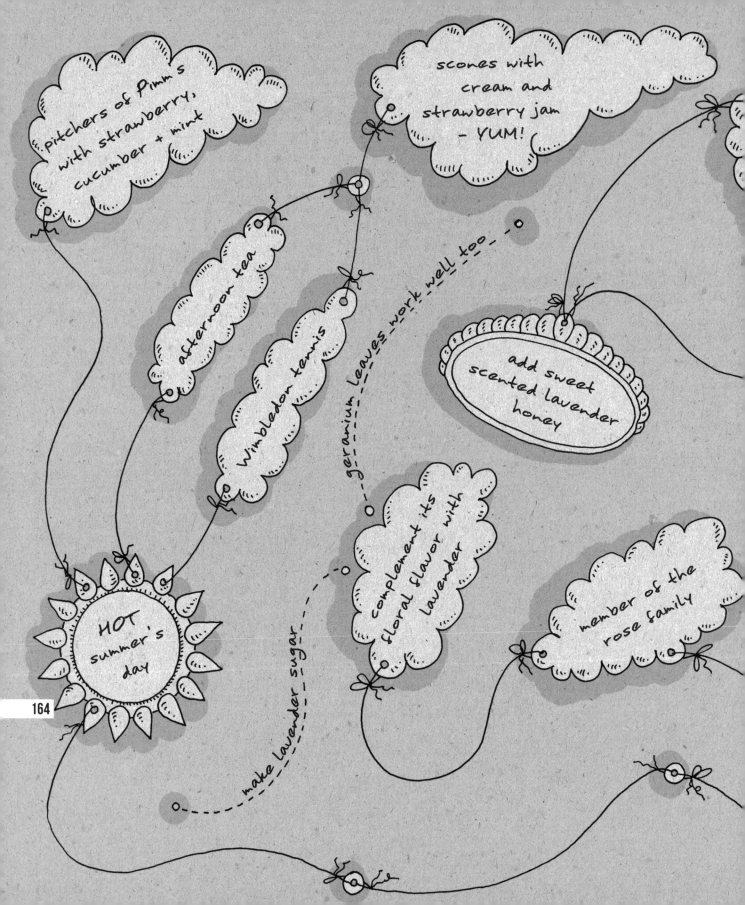

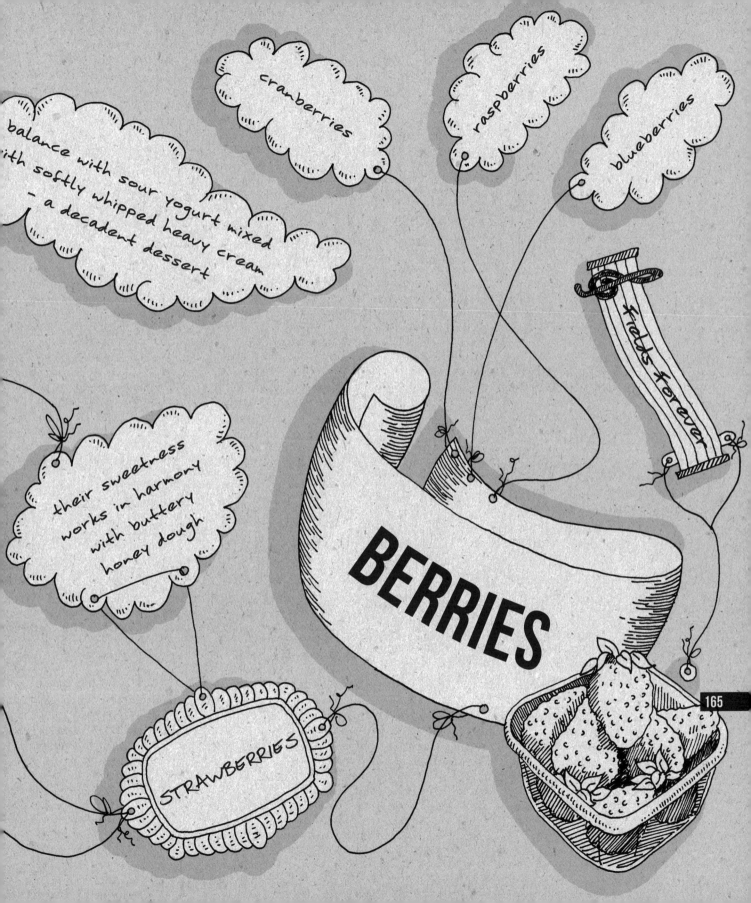

cranberries

raspberries

blueberries

balance with sour yogurt mixed with softly whipped heavy cream – a decadent dessert

fields forever

their sweetness works in harmony with buttery honey dough

BERRIES

STRAWBERRIES

Blueberries are popular for breakfast, as is coffee. So one day I got to thinking, why not combine the two ingredients in a muffin? The coffee flavor is really subtle and works surprisingly well. < MAKES 6–8 >

BLUEBERRY AND COFFEE MUFFINS

Preheat the oven to 400°F. Line a six-cup muffin pan with six 4 x 4in squares of parchment paper.

Sift the flour and baking powder together in a bowl, then stir in the sugar.

In another bowl, whisk together the eggs, coffee, milk, and oil. Pour the liquid ingredients into the flour mixture, add the blueberries, and stir until just combined. (Overmixing will result in heavy muffins.)

Spoon the mixture into the prepared muffin pan, place on a baking sheet, and cook in the oven for 25 minutes or until golden and cooked through. Test by inserting the point of a knife to see if it comes out clean.

Leave to cool for 5 minutes in the pan before turning out onto a wire rack to cool completely. Serve the muffins in their paper "jackets."

2⅓ cups all-purpose flour
1 tbsp baking powder
½ cup sugar
2 eggs, lightly beaten
4 tsp instant coffee, dissolved in 1 tbsp boiling water
¾ cup milk
¾ cup light olive oil
6oz blueberries, fresh or frozen

Tart and spicy! Use the jelly as an accompaniment to sweet and savory dishes. Great with oily fish such as mackerel, as well as goat cheese and pork and lamb; or swirl through chocolate brownies or ice cream to add surprise.

CRANBERRY CHILLI JELLY

2½lb cranberries

1 red chilli pepper, finely chopped (add the seeds if you like it spicy!)

1lb sugar per 20fl oz cranberry juice

sterilized jam jars, warmed in the oven at 200°F for 30 minutes

parchment paper

You will need sterilized jam jars to store your cranberry jelly, so warm some clean jars in the oven at 225°F for 30 minutes.

Wash the cranberries and sort through them, discarding any that are damaged. Place in a heavy-bottomed saucepan and cover with water. Bring to a boil, then reduce to a simmer and cook until the cranberry skins split.

Crush the fruit a little with a potato masher, then pour into a jelly bag or a sieve lined with muslin and strain for 3–4 hours or overnight. Place a small plate or saucer in the freezer for later.

Measure the cranberry juice and heat in a pan with sugar. Add 2¼ cups sugar to every 2 cups juice. Discard the cranberries. Heat the juice and sugar in a saucepan, stirring until the sugar is completely dissolved.

Bring to a boil and cook rapidly, removing any foam, until the jelly sets when tested. (Test by pouring a little onto your chilled plate or saucer; leave for 30 seconds or so, push the jelly a little, and see if it's set. If not, cook for a little longer and test again frequently.)

Pour the jelly into the warmed sterilized jars, cover with a circle of parchment paper, and seal when cool. Store in a cool place away from direct sunlight.

VARIATIONS

- Serve with pan-fried mackerel (see recipe #35), buttered new potatoes and a salad for a delicious lunch or light dinner after a hard day's fishing!
- Why not use the discarded cranberries and chilli to infuse vodka? Strain and serve in a cocktail with mint, apple juice and lime.

168

I used to dislike rosewater as a kid, but I've since learned to love its delicate perfumed flavor. I think the sourness of the mascarpone and yogurt complements the sweetness of the meringues better than whipped cream. < SERVES 4 >

MIDDLE EASTERN INSPIRED ETON MESS

Whisk together the mascarpone, Greek yogurt, confectioners' sugar, and rosewater. Set aside in the refrigerator if using later.

Put the strawberries in a bowl and gently crush about one third of them with the end of a rolling pin. Add the meringues, Turkish delight, almonds, and mint. Fold in the mascarpone cream and serve in individual glasses or bowls.

VARIATIONS

- Try replacing the rosewater with orange flower water and use ripe chopped apricots instead of the strawberries.
- Use a different flavored Turkish delight or another kind of the nut. For example you could try orange flower Turkish delight with pistachios.

7oz mascarpone

½ cup Greek yogurt

½ cup confectioners' sugar, sifted

1 tbsp rosewater

7oz ripe strawberries, hulled

2 large meringues, broken into rough pieces

4 cubes rose-flavored Turkish delight, diced

½ cup skin-on almonds, chopped

8 mint leaves, shredded

Don't worry if you can't find lavender or lavender honey; it'll be just as delicious without! You can prepare the dough two days in advance. Then either cook to order or reheat the cooked dough in the oven. < SERVES 4 >

LAVENDER HONEY DOUGH
WITH CRUSHED STRAWBERRIES, YOGURT, AND CREAM

FOR THE DOUGH

1 whole egg plus 3 yolks

¼ cup Lavender Sugar (recipe #110) or 2 tbsp gently warmed lavender honey

2 tbsp unsalted butter, melted

4 tbsp honey or lavender honey

1¾ cups all-purpose flour

¼ tsp baking soda

½ tsp baking powder

1 cup heavy cream

1½ cups Greek yogurt

1lb strawberries, hulled and quartered

¼ cup Lavender Sugar (or just use superfine sugar)

vegetable or grapeseed oil, for frying

To make the dough, whisk together the whole egg, egg yolks, and the lavender sugar, if using, until pale. Whisk in the butter and honey, if using. Sift in the flour, baking soda, baking powder, and mix until the dough comes together. Turn out onto a lightly floured surface and knead to form a smooth and elastic dough. (If you have a food processor, use the dough hook for this.) Wrap the dough in plastic wrap and leave to rest in a cool place for 30 minutes.

Lightly flour a work surface, roll out the dough to about $\frac{1}{16}$in thick, and cut into twelve 3in diamonds or rectangles. Place on a lightly flour-dusted sheet of parchment paper and refrigerate until ready to use.

Whisk the cream to form soft peaks, then fold in the yogurt. Refrigerate until required.

Place the strawberries in a bowl and lightly crush with a fork. Sprinkle with the lavender sugar and leave to macerate.

To cook the honey dough, pour the oil into a frying pan until it's ¾–1¼in deep and heat to 350°F or until a square of bread turns golden in 30 seconds. Fry the honey dough in batches for 1–2 minutes on either side or until golden and puffed. Remove with a slotted spoon and drain on paper towels.

To assemble, pile the cream and strawberries on top of the honey dough, drizzle with honey, and repeat with another layer. Alternatively, serve separately and allow your guests to assemble their own.

VARIATIONS

- Use any seasonal berry and use the mascarpone yogurt cream recipe that goes with the Eton Mess (recipe #82).
- Omit the fruit and scatter the dough with roasted nuts and sprinkle with honey of your choice.

A British retro classic with a twist. I am on a mission to reinvent the arctic roll and take it to new heights! By the way, you'll need to make the ice cream in advance with the aid of an ice cream maker. < SERVES 4 >

RASPBERRY, AMARETTI, AND GREEK YOGURT ICE CREAM ARCTIC ROLL

To make the ice cream, whisk the cream, milk, milk powder, and sugar together and pour into a saucepan. Bring to a boil, then remove from the heat and leave to cool. Whisk in the yogurt and churn in an ice-cream maker. After 10 minutes, add the raspberries and amaretti cookies and continue to churn until frozen. Spoon the ice cream onto a sheet of parchment paper, then roll up and mold into a 2 x 12in sausage and freeze until solid.

Preheat the oven to 375°F and line a 10 x 13in Swiss roll pan with parchment paper.

To make the sponge cake, whisk together the eggs and sugar until pale and thickened. Sift the flour over the mixture and fold in. Pour into the prepared pan, smooth with a spatula, and cook for 10–12 minutes or until just firm to the touch.

Place a sheet of parchment paper that's slightly bigger than the tray onto a work surface and dust with superfine sugar. Turn the cake out and peel away the parchment. Set aside to cool slightly.

To assemble, spread the raspberry jam over the sponge, leaving a ¾in gap around the edge. Remove the parchment paper from the ice-cream sausage and place the ice cream along the long side of the cake. Using the parchment paper to help you, roll up the sponge so the ice cream is encased. To serve, cut into slices and garnish with fresh raspberries.

FOR THE ICE CREAM
⅓ cup heavy cream
⅓ cup milk
1oz nonfat dry milk powder
¾ cup superfine sugar
1¾ cups Greek yogurt
1¼ cups raspberries, fresh or frozen
10 amaretti cookies, coarsely crushed

FOR THE SPONGE CAKE
3 eggs
⅓ cup superfine sugar
⅔ cup self-rising flour
5 tbsp raspberry jam,

16 fresh raspberries, to serve

VARIATIONS

- Stir Turkish delight through the ice cream or swirl through some raspberry purée.
- Try serving with a rich chocolate sauce. Substitute raspberries for diced mango or peaches for a twist on peach melba.
- Substitute ⅓ cup flour for ground almonds for a nuttier flavor.

silky soft and smooth

Provence

combine with lavender

one of the first signs of summer

creamy + floral

good with cardamom

APRICOTS

roast with Earl Grey tea

the pit tastes similar to almonds

or cook in dessert wine (Riesling) and serve with blue cheese

frangipane is a creamy filling made from almonds

but don't eat too many - they contain cyanide!

chocolate pastry, frangipane, and fresh cherries - combined in a tart

affinity for dairy – cream, ice cream, goat cheese, blue cheese

serve with cilantro couscous

harmonious with fatty, flavor-loaded duck

PEACHES

vanilla

STONE FRUIT

plums

the bark and stems of wild cherries have a scent of almonds

LOLA!

cherry cola

earrings

CHERRIES

Cherry Ripe = Australian chocolate bar with cherries + coconut

cherries dipped in chocolate – bliss!

good with sour goat cheese

Soft, ripe spiced peaches, sticky cardamom-scented braised duck, aromatic couscous, and peppery watercress provide a feast for the season. Perfect for a lazy late summer dinner. < SERVES 4 >

SLOW-BRAISED DUCK WITH COUSCOUS AND CUMIN ROASTED PEACHES

FOR THE DUCK
1 onion, peeled and sliced
1 red chile, coarsely chopped
2 carrots, coarsely chopped
2 celery ribs, coarsely chopped
2 quarts chicken stock
2 cinnamon sticks
15 cardamom pods
pinch of saffron
4 star anise
4 garlic cloves
⅓ cup honey
4 small duck legs

FOR THE COUSCOUS
1¾ cups instant couscous
4 tbsp butter, diced
2 tbsp raisins
2 tbsp pine nuts, toasted
sea salt and black pepper

FOR THE CUMIN ROASTED PEACHES
2 peaches, quartered
2 tbsp demerara (brown) sugar
1 tbsp cumin seeds
1 tbsp ground cumin
2 tbsp butter

Place the onion, chile, carrots, celery, and stock in a large pan. Add the cinnamon sticks, cardamom pods, saffron, star anise, garlic, and honey. Bring to a simmer.

Add the duck legs to the stock. Cover with a circle of parchment paper, carefully pressing it down onto the surface of the liquid, then top with a plate that just fits inside the pan. This helps the duck to cook evenly. Simmer gently for about 1½–2 hours or until the duck legs are tender.

Remove the duck legs and set aside. Strain the cooking liquid through a sieve and skim the fat from the surface or, if preparing in advance, leave to cool then refrigerate the liquor overnight with the duck legs. The next day, remove the hard fat that has settled on the surface.

Preheat the oven to 425°F.

Heat the cooking liquid until boiling. Ladle 1 cup of the hot liquid into a pitcher to use for the couscous, then continue boiling the remaining liquid until it has reduced by half and thickened to a sauce.

Place the couscous in a large heatproof bowl with the butter and raisins; heat the cooking liquid set aside and pour over the couscous. Cover the bowl immediately with plastic wrap and leave for 3 minutes. Remove the plastic wrap, fluff up the grains with a fork, then add the pine nuts, season with salt and pepper, and set aside.

To prepare the peaches, toss them with the sugar and both types of cumin. Place a frying pan over high heat and when it is hot, add the butter and peaches. Cook until the peaches are soft and caramelized, shaking the pan occasionally.

Reheat the duck legs on a baking sheet in the hot oven. Just before serving, place them under a preheated broiler to caramelize the skin. Serve the duck legs in deep bowls with the peaches and sauce, with the couscous on the side.

176

A simple, easily adapted recipe for roasting apricots. I first thought about using tea bags after my good friend Carrie Anne told me she'd used a mint tea bag to flavor her risotto when she'd forgotten to buy fresh. < SERVES 4 >

EARL GREY ROASTED APRICOTS

½ cup sugar
1 Earl Grey tea bag
8 apricots, unpeeled, halved, and pitted

Preheat the oven to 350°F.

Place the sugar and ⅓ cup + 1 tablespoon water in a small saucepan and bring to a boil. Add the tea bag and simmer for 5 minutes until syrupy.

Place the apricots cut-side down in a small roasting pan or ovenproof dish. Remove the tea bag from the syrup, pour the syrup over the apricots, and roast for about 10 minutes. Turn the apricots over and baste with the syrup, then roast for another 5 minutes or until tender.

Serve hot or cold for breakfast, with Masala Chai Rice Pudding (recipe #75). Also delicious with anything chocolatey, goat cheese, or meringues.

VARIATIONS

- Take this recipe on a flavor journey by changing the flavor of the tea bags—ginger and lemon tea bags would work equally well, as would various herbal flavors. You could even add a vanilla bean or omit the tea altogether.

178

There's nothing better than a simple fruit fool. Here's the basic recipe, but you can adapt it as you wish (see variations below). Plums are excellent partnered with ginger, cardamom, and cinnamon. < SERVES 4 >

PLUM FOOL

Cut the plums in half and remove the pits, then cut into quarters and place in a pan with 2 tablespoons water and the sugar. Cook over low heat until the plums have broken down and are meltingly soft (about 10–20 minutes, depending on how ripe the plums are). Discard any skins that have separated.

Place in a blender and process to a smooth purée. Leave to cool, then refrigerate until you're ready to make the fool.

Place the cream and vanilla seeds in a bowl and whisk to form soft peaks. Fold in a third of the cooled plums, followed by the remainder. Pour into bowls or glasses and chill for 20 minutes before serving.

1lb 2oz plums
½ cup superfine sugar, plus extra to taste
⅔ cup heavy cream
1 vanilla bean, halved and scraped of seeds

VARIATIONS

- Stem ginger folded through this fool is delicious.
- Try folding in crumbled amaretti cookies.
- For a lighter dessert, use half the cream and make up the balance with Greek yogurt, folded in.
- I love marzipan, especially those chocolate-covered bars you sometimes find. Try chopping those up and adding to your plum fool—delicious!
- Replace the figs in the Dried Fig and Polenta Cookies (recipe #109) with chopped prunes for a perfect accompaniment.

Inspired by the Australian chocolate bar, "Cherry Ripe," this crisp, dark chocolate pastry case is filled with a light coconut frangipane and studded with morello cherries. Serve with a cup of tea, or with ice cream. < SERVES 8–12 >

#88

CHERRY RIPE TART

Place the butter, flour, sugar, cocoa, and salt in a food processor and process until the mixture resembles bread crumbs. With the motor still running, add the egg yolks and milk until the mixture comes together, adding a little more milk if necessary. Wrap the dough in plastic wrap and refrigerate for 1 hour or overnight.

Sprinkle a work surface with flour and roll the pastry out into a circle just slightly larger than a 10in tart pan. Line the pan with the pastry, trim off any excess, and refrigerate for at least 15 minutes.

To make the coconut frangipane, cream the butter and confectioners' sugar together, then gradually whisk in the eggs. Fold in the almonds, the coconut, and the flour.

Preheat the oven to 350°F.

Line the pastry shell with parchment paper and baking beans and bake blind for 15 minutes. Remove the paper and the beans and bake for another 5 minutes. Remove from the oven, spoon the jam over the pastry base, top with the coconut frangipane, then stud the tart with the whole pitted cherries. Bake for 30–40 minutes until the frangipane has set and is golden. Leave to cool a little before serving.

VARIATIONS

- Serve the tart with cherry compote and chocolate sauce if liked. Garnish with whole cherries.

FOR THE CHOCOLATE PASTRY

12 tbsp (1½ cups) cold unsalted butter, cut into small cubes

1¾ cups all-purpose flour, sifted, plus extra for dusting

⅓ cup superfine sugar

⅔ cup unsweetened cocoa powder

pinch of sea salt

2 egg yolks

3 tbsp milk

FOR THE COCONUT FRANGIPANE

9 tbsp unsalted butter, diced

1 cup confectioners' sugar

3 eggs

¾ cup ground almonds

¾ cup unsweetened coconut flakes

¼ cup all-purpose flour

3 tbsp morello cherry jam

1½lb fresh cherries, pitted (leave a few with stems) or 1 can morello cherries, well drained

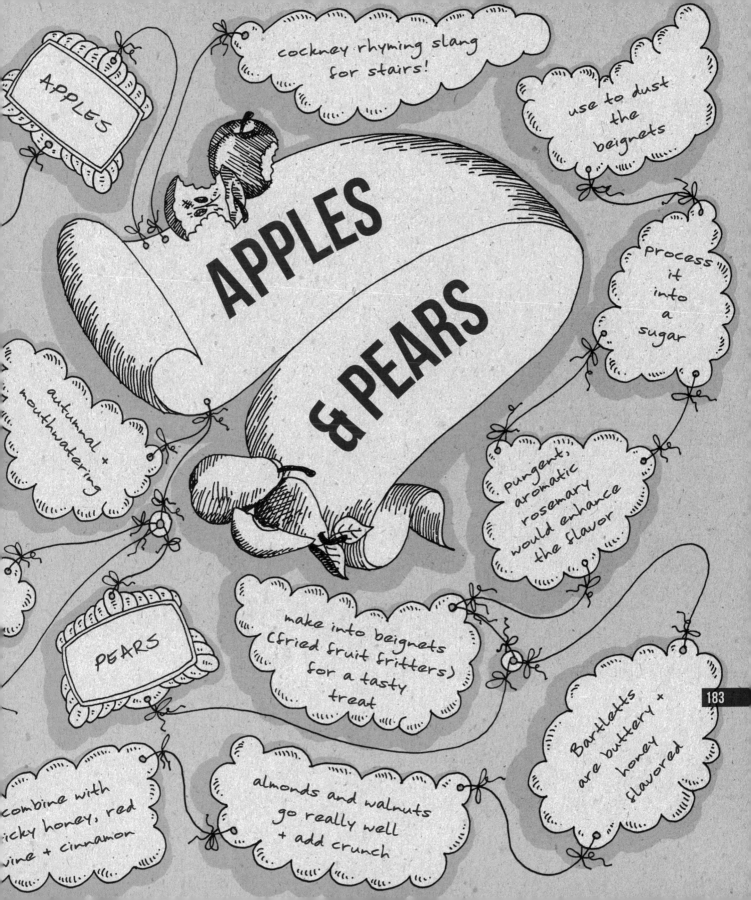

A great brunch recipe: plump juicy scallops wrapped in smoky pancetta, drizzled with maple syrup, sitting on delicate apple pancakes. You will need eight toothpicks for this. < SERVES 4 >

APPLE BUCKWHEAT PANCAKES WITH SCALLOPS, PANCETTA, AND CRÈME FRAÎCHE

FOR THE PANCAKES
1²/₃ cups all-purpose flour
¾ cup buckwheat flour
pinch of sea salt
2 tsp baking powder
2 eggs, beaten
1 cup + 2 tbsp apple juice
⅓ cup honey
1 tbsp olive oil
1 apple, peeled, cored, and coarsely grated
2 tbsp butter

FOR THE APPLES
1 apple, peeled, cored and cut into eighths
1 tbsp superfine sugar

FOR THE SCALLOPS
4 slices smoked pancetta
8 scallops, roe removed
sea salt and black pepper
1 tbsp olive oil
4 tbsp maple syrup

TO SERVE
handful of baby spinach leaves
4 tbsp crème fraîche

Sift the flours, salt, and baking powder into a bowl. Beat the eggs with the apple juice, honey, and oil. Using an electric whisk, add the liquid ingredients to the flour mixture and blend until smooth. Stir in the apple.

Heat a little butter in a non-stick frying pan. Spoon 1 heaping tablespoon of the pancake mix into the pan and cook over medium heat for about 2 minutes or until golden on each side. Remove and repeat with the remaining batter. Leave in a warm place.

Next, prepare the apple mixture. Toss the apple pieces in the sugar. Preheat a frying pan over medium heat, add the apple, and allow the sugar to caramelize and the apples to soften (about 2 minutes). Transfer to a plate or tray and leave to cool.

Next, cut the pancetta in half widthwise. Season the scallops with sea salt and pepper and wrap in pancetta, securing each with a toothpick.

Heat the olive oil in the frying pan. Once hot, add the scallops and cook over medium heat for 2 minutes, until the pancetta is crisp. Drizzle with maple syrup and heat through. Alternatively, you can place the scallops under a preheated broiler and cook for 2–3 minutes on each side.

To serve, place the pancakes on a plate, top each one with a little baby spinach, a blob of crème fraîche, some apple mixture, and two scallops. Drizzle with the pan juices and maple syrup and serve immediately, topped with freshly ground black pepper.

VARIATIONS

• Try using banana in place of the scallops!

An alternative to everyone's favorite–apple pie. Sour Macintosh apples combine with sweet woody cinnamon and ginger. All brought together with creamy mascarpone cheese–absolutely gorgeous! < SERVES 8–10 >

BAKED MACINTOSH APPLE CHEESECAKE

You will need a non-stick springform cake pan, about 10in in diameter and lined with parchment paper.

Heat a large frying pan. Toss the apple pieces with the superfine sugar and cinnamon, then pour into the frying pan. The sugar will caramelize as soon as it hits the hot pan. Shake the pan a little to stop the apples from burning, and cook over high heat until caramelized, for no more than 2 minutes. Remove from the heat and transfer the apples onto a plate or tray to cool.

Preheat the oven to 350°F.

Place the gingersnaps in a food processor and process to make crumbs. Slowly add the melted butter and mix until combined. Pour into the bottom of the cake pan and press down with the back of a spoon until even. Top the cookie base with the apples and scatter with raisins.

Whisk the eggs and sugar together until pale, add the cream cheese, mascarpone, and stem ginger, and gently whisk, making sure not to overmix or it will separate. Pour the mixture over the apples, place the pan on a baking sheet, and cook in the oven for about 50–70 minutes until the cheesecake wobbles a little. Turn off the heat and leave the oven door ajar for 20 minutes; the cake will continue to cook and this will prevent the top from cracking.

Remove the cake from the oven, leave to cool, then refrigerate until required. Remove from the fridge 20 minutes before serving.

For the apple chips, preheat the oven to 230°F. Using a mandolin, slice the apple vertically as thinly as possible, and place in a single layer on a baking sheet lined with parchment paper. Sprinkle with sugar and bake for 1½–2 hours until crisp. Loosen the chips with an offset spatula and leave to cool. Store in an airtight container until required (these can be made a few days ahead if you like).

Garnish the cheesecake with the apple chips. This is wonderful served with a spoonful of Calvados crème fraîche!

FOR THE APPLES
2 Macintosh apples, peeled, cored, and cut into ½in pieces

¼ cup superfine sugar

1 heaping tsp cinnamon

FOR THE CHEESECAKE
1 package gingersnap cookies

4 tbsp butter, melted

1-2 tsp raisins, soaked in hot water and drained

5 eggs

¾ cup superfine sugar

14oz cream cheese

14oz mascarpone

2 tbsp of stem ginger, finely chopped

FOR THE APPLE CHIP GARNISH
1 Macintosh apple

¼ cup superfine sugar

A recipe inspired by British chololatier Paul A. Young. When I met him he was cooking a poached pear, which he then dipped in a chocolate and Stilton ganache! Paul's passion for chocolate is totally inspirational. < SERVES 4 >

CHOCOLATE-DIPPED POACHED PEARS, STUFFED WITH STICKY NUTS

FOR THE STICKY NUTS
2 tbsp honey
½ cinnamon stick
¼ cup walnut halves, toasted
2½ tbsp blanched almonds, toasted

FOR THE PEAR POACHING LIQUID
zest and juice of 1 orange
1 cinnamon stick
1¼ cups sugar
2½ cups red wine
4 firm pears

FOR THE GANACHE
3½oz dark chocolate (70 percent cocoa solids)
½ cup heavy cream
pinch of ground cinnamon

To make the sticky nuts, place the honey, 3 tablespoons water, and the cinnamon stick in a small saucepan and bring to a boil. Reduce the heat and simmer until thickened. Leave to cool and discard the cinnamon stick.

Pulse the nuts in a food processor or crush to a coarse bread crumb texture and mix with the syrup.

To make the poached pears, place the orange zest and juice, the cinnamon stick, sugar, and red wine in a saucepan just big enough to hold the pears. Place over medium heat and bring to a boil.

Peel the pears and, using an apple corer or melon baller, remove enough of the core from the bottom end to create a cavity for the nuts. Leave the stems intact and place in the hot poaching liquid. Cover with a piece of parchment paper and simmer for about 15–20 minutes or until the pears are tender, but holding their shape.

Preheat the oven to 400°F.

Remove the pears from the poaching liquid and set aside to cool. Reduce the liquid to a syrup, then leave to cool at room temperature.

Pat the pears dry with paper towels, then stuff each one with the sticky nuts, leveling the bottom with a knife so the pears stand upright. Place on a non-stick baking sheet and bake in the oven for 10 minutes. Remove from the oven and leave to rest for 5 minutes.

To make the ganache, place the chocolate, cream, and cinnamon in a small heatproof bowl set over a pan of simmering water. Once melted, set aside and leave to cool a little before dipping and rolling each pear in the ganache to coat it halfway up. Place on parchment paper, cool, and refrigerate until required.

Serve with a little of the poaching liquid and a dollop of Greek yogurt or crème fraîche.

I once worked with Jen Beer, a quirky young Australian chef with a huge heart. Jen used to lovingly prepare us all Bircher muesli and it soon became a kitchen favorite. A wonderful healthy way to start the day. < SERVES 4 >

BIRCHER MUESLI WITH GRATED APPLE

Mix together all the ingredients, cover, and refrigerate for 2 hours or, preferably, overnight. Serve chilled, drizzled with honey or agave nectar.

VARIATIONS

- You can really experiment with Bircher muesli. Whichever journey you choose to take your muesli on I'm sure you'll agree it's a fabulous breakfast and it will happily sit in the fridge for three days.

- Vary the dried fruits used here and substitute with dried cranberries, cherries, or blueberries.

- Use a mix of seeds such as flax seed, sunflower, and pumpkin.

- Grated pear and pear juice make a great alternative to apple and both provide a natural sweetness, so no need to add any extra.

- Top with fresh berries if in season or serve swirled with flavorful rhubarb compote.

1 cup rolled oats

½ cup good-quality apple juice

¼ cup golden raisins

¼ cup dried apricots, chopped

1 Granny Smith apple, unpeeled, coarsely grated

1 cup Greek yogurt

¼ cup pumpkin seeds

3 tbsp toasted almond flakes, coarsely chopped

pinch of freshly ground nutmeg

½ tsp ground cinnamon

Tasty pear fritters! Robust pears are just "pearfect" with rosemary scented sugar—make this in advance if you can, you will find all sorts of uses for it. A little lager in the batter really does improve the taste. < SERVES 4—6 >

PEAR BEIGNETS WITH ROSEMARY SUGAR AND PEAR CRÈME ANGLAISE

FOR THE POACHED PEARS

1 cup superfine sugar
1 bay leaf
1 vanilla bean, seeds scraped
1 whole unwaxed lemon
4 pears, peeled and cored

FOR THE BATTER

1¼ cups all-purpose flour
3 tbsp sugar
pinch of sea salt
1 large egg
¾ cup lager or ale
vegetable oil, for frying
confectioners' sugar

FOR THE PEAR CRÈME ANGLAISE

⅓ cup + 1 tbsp milk
⅓ cup light cream
2 egg yolks
1 tbsp superfine sugar

FOR THE ROSEMARY SUGAR

2 sprigs of rosemary, dried, leaves stripped
⅓ cup superfine sugar

Prepare the poaching liquid before preparing the pears, as they discolor. Place the sugar, ½ cup water, bay leaf, vanilla seeds and bean, bay leaf, and the juice and the lemon in a saucepan over low heat and bring to a boil for 2 minutes.

Cut each pear into 3—4 vertical slices about ½in thick and add to the cooking liquid. Place a circle of parchment paper (a cartouche) on the top and poach until just tender (about 5—7 minutes). Remove the pears from the liquid and leave to cool and drain on a rack or cloth.

In a medium bowl, combine the flour, sugar, a pinch of salt, and the egg. Whisk together and gradually add the lager or ale. Whisk until the batter is smooth. Leave to rest for 10 minutes.

To make the rosemary sugar, process the rosemary and sugar together in a blender. Store in an airtight container until required.

Heat the oil to 325°F. Working in batches, dip a few slices of poached pear into the batter, then carefully drop them into the oil. Fry until golden on both sides (about 4 minutes).

Drain the pear beignets on absorbent paper towels and dust with rosemary sugar.

To make the pear crème anglaise, place 50ml of the pear poaching syrup, the milk and cream in a saucepan and gently bring to a boil.

In a separate bowl, whisk the egg yolks and sugar until pale. Pour a little of the hot milk mixture into the egg mixture, then gradually pour this back into the hot milk. Cook over low heat, stirring continuously until the custard thickens. Do not boil or the custard will curdle. Once thickened, pass the custard through a fine sieve and serve with the pears.

Pomelos look like huge grapefruits. Their thick skin and membrane can be ripped away to reveal a segmented fruit with a dense texture, sometimes sweet, a little dry, tart, and fruity. < SERVES 4 AS A SIDE SALAD >

#94

POMELO AND LIME LEAF SALAD WITH *NAM JIM* DRESSING

Break the pomelo into segments and tear each one in half into a bowl. Add the remaining ingredients, then chill in the fridge until required.

To make the dressing, pound the garlic and cilantro roots in a mortar and pestle until well crushed, but not to a paste. Add the chiles and crush lightly, then mix in the palm sugar, followed by the fish sauce and lime juice.

Balance the flavors: if a little too salty, add a bit more lime; if too sour, add a splash more fish sauce. Fifty percent fish sauce to lime juice should give you the perfect balance.

Just before serving, toss the salad with the *nam jim* and serve immediately.

VARIATIONS

- For a delicious main course, fry or grill some peeled shrimp and toss into the salad.
- If watermelons are in season, add a few chunks, some mint leaves, a few roasted peanuts, and some sliced scallions. Dress and serve at once.
- Alternatively, grill a rib-eye steak until rare, leave to rest, then slice and toss with the pomelo salad ingredients and any of the ingredients from the shrimp suggestion above. To give it some bulk, add some cooked glass or rice noodles.
- Try with some shredded chicken or crabmeat or grilled or pan-fried squid. Or use the dressing spooned over freshly shucked oysters.
- If you can get ahold of some green papaya, peel and thinly shred it, then mix with the *nam jim* dressing, some dried shrimp, halved cherry tomatoes, roasted peanuts, shredded ginger, scallions, and a handful of cilantro, mint, and Thai basil leaves—a salad I used to eat every day for lunch in Thailand.

2 pomelos

2 lime leaves, stems removed, finely shredded

handful of cilantro, coarsely chopped

1 red chile, seeded and finely sliced

¾in piece of fresh ginger or galangal, peeled and finely chopped or julienned

few Thai basil leaves (optional), torn

FOR THE *NAM JIM* DRESSING

2 garlic cloves

4 cilantro roots, washed and coarsely chopped

1–2 red chiles (depending on their heat), seeded and coarsely chopped

2 tbsp palm sugar

2 tbsp Thai fish sauce

¼ cup fresh lime juice

195

A fantastic, simple summer salad—other than the jelly and dressing, it's more an assembly job than anything else. The zingy jelly cuts through the rich cheese (it also goes very well in a sandwich with cold roast pork). < SERVES 4 >

BLUE CHEESE, PEAR, CAPICOLA, LEMON, AND GINGER JELLY AND BITTER LEAF SALAD

FOR THE JELLY

1oz fresh ginger, peeled and finely grated

zest of 1 lemon

3 tbsp fresh lemon juice

2 tbsp superfine sugar

½ tsp agar agar

FOR THE WHITE WINE DRESSING

1 tbsp olive oil

1 tbsp extra virgin olive oil

1 tbso Chardonnay vinegar (if unavailable, use white wine vinegar)

FOR THE SALAD

¾oz mizuna or other mixed bitter leaves

1 head dandelion, leaves picked in 2in lengths and washed

3oz blue cheese, thinly sliced

1 pear, cored, quartered and thinly sliced

12 slices capicola

freshly ground black pepper

First make the jelly. Put the ginger, lemon zest and juice, and sugar in a saucepan, add ⅔ cup water, and bring to a boil over low heat. The moment it starts boiling, lower the heat, whisk in the agar agar, and cook for 1 minute. Tip into a shallow container and leave to cool before covering and refrigerating. You can make the jelly up to 3 days in advance. (These quantities make more than you need, but it will keep quite happily in the fridge for up to a week.)

Next, make the dressing by lightly whisking together the oils and vinegar.

To assemble, scatter the leaves in a narrow line on four plates, top with slices of cheese and pear, followed by slivers of jelly. Top with capicola, drizzle with dressing, grind over a little black pepper, and serve.

You could make just the ice cream or the madeleines if you prefer, but if you really want to go to town with lemon verbena, make both! Glazed madeleines are best left uncovered and eaten the day they're made. < SERVES 4 >

#96

LEMON VERBENA ICE CREAM WITH GLAZED MADELEINES

Place the lemon verbena leaves in a heavy-bottomed saucepan with the milk and cream and gently bring to just below boiling point. Remove from the heat, cover, and leave to infuse for 2 hours or overnight.

To make the ice cream, gently reheat the infused milk mixture to boiling point again. Meanwhile, whisk the sugar and egg yolks until pale. Once the milk is hot, slowly pour it over the yolks and sugar, whisking continuously. Pour the mixture back into the saucepan and cook, stirring all the time, over low heat until the custard coats the back of the spoon. (If you are using a thermometer, it should read 175–185°F). Immediately strain the custard through a sieve into a large bowl, pushing down on the verbena leaves to extract as much flavor as possible. Leave to cool, then freeze in an ice-cream maker, according to the manufacturer's instructions.

For the madeleines, melt the butter in a saucepan over low heat, remove from the heat, and add the verbena leaves. Leave to infuse for 10 minutes. Sift the flour, baking powder, and salt into a medium-sized bowl. Using an electric mixer, beat the eggs and sugar together until thick, light, and fluffy. Add the honey and lemon zest and beat for another minute. Gently fold in the dry ingredients by hand, followed by the verbena-flavored butter. Press plastic wrap directly onto the surface of the batter and chill for at least 3 hours or overnight.

Preheat the oven to 400°F. Thoroughly grease a madeleine pan with 12 indentations. Dust with flour and tap out the excess. Or use a silicone Madeleine tray. Place the pan on a baking sheet. Drop a large tablespoon of batter into each mold (don't smooth out, as it will spread during baking). Place on the middle rack of the oven and bake until golden (about 10 minutes) or until a skewer inserted into the center comes out clean. If using a pan, tap on a work surface to loosen the cakes before turning them out onto a wire rack to cool slightly before glazing.

To make the glaze, stir all the ingredients together in a small mixing bowl until smooth. The moment the madeleines are cool enough to handle, dip each one in the glaze and rest on the cooking rack until the glaze has set.

Serve the madeleines with the ice cream.

FOR THE ICE CREAM

½oz fresh lemon verbena leaves or 2 lemon verbena tea bags

1 cup + 3 tbsp milk

⅔ cup heavy cream

¾ cup sugar

4 egg yolks

FOR THE MADELEINES

5 tbsp unsalted butter, plus extra for greasing

4 tbsp fresh, finely chopped lemon verbena or 2 tbsp dried leaves or lemon verbena tea

¾ cup all-purpose flour, plus extra for dusting

½ tsp baking powder

pinch of sea salt

2 large eggs

⅓ cup sugar

2 tbsp honey

½ tsp grated lemon zest

FOR THE LEMON VERBENA GLAZE

1⅓ cups confectioners' sugar

1 tbsp freshly squeezed lemon juice

3 tbsp finely chopped lemon verbena or 1 tbsp dried

2 tbsp water

199

A little bit of Italy frozen and encased in a meringue coat—this is a classic dessert, spruced up for the 21st Century. The explosion of cool and refreshing lemon really wakes up the taste buds. < SERVES 6–8 >

LIMONCELLO BAKED ALASKA

FOR THE LEMON AND LIME CAKE

8oz (2 sticks) unsalted butter

1 cup superfine sugar

4 eggs, beaten

1¾ cups self-rising flour

zest of 2 lemons, finely grated

juice of 1 lemon

¼ cup limoncello, plus more for layering

FOR THE ICE CREAM

8 scoops (about 10½oz) vanilla ice cream

8 tbsp lemon curd

FOR THE MERINGUE

6 egg whites

1¼ cups superfine sugar

24 fresh lychees, peeled (or 1 can)

4 lime leaves, finely chopped (optional)

Preheat the oven to 350°F. Grease and line a 8½ x 4½in loaf pan.

Cream together the butter and sugar until pale and creamy. Gradually whisk in the eggs. Sift in the flour, add the lemon zest, and fold to combine. Add the lemon juice and pour the batter into the prepared pan. Bake in the oven for 45–50 minutes or until a skewer inserted in the center comes out clean. Leave to cool a little before turning out onto a wire rack.

Once cool, cut the cake horizontally into three slices.

Grease then line the loaf pan with plastic wrap, so it overhangs. Place a layer of cake in the bottom and drizzle with the limoncello.

Soften the ice cream a little and beat in the lemon curd. Spread half of the ice cream over the cake. Top with another layer of cake, again dousing in limoncello, followed by the remaining ice cream. Smooth the surface before topping with the remaining cake layer, again dousing in limoncello. Freeze until rock hard. (Note: you can make this step up to a week ahead, then cover with plastic wrap until required.)

Preheat the oven to 400°F.

Place the egg whites in a clean, grease-free bowl. Whisk to form soft peaks, then gradually whisk in the sugar until the meringue is stiff and shiny. (You can make this ahead of time and leave it in the fridge for a couple of hours).

Remove the cake from the pan, using the plastic wrap to help. Turn out onto an ovenproof serving dish. Top the cake with a thick layer of meringue, forming peaks and swirls as you go. Make sure the cake is completely covered. Bake for 3–4 minutes, or until meringue is slightly toasted.

Serve immediately with lychees and finely chopped lime leaves for a refreshing accompaniment.

A refreshing sorbet to serve after dinner. Use the zests to make a Pink Grapefruit Vodka (see below) which in turn can be poured over the sorbet.

< SERVES 4–6 >

PINK GRAPEFRUIT AND TARRAGON SORBET

Put the sugar, ⅔ cup water, and tarragon stems in a small saucepan over low heat and heat gently until the sugar has dissolved. Remove from the heat and leave to infuse for 1 hour.

Strain the liquid, then add the grapefruit juice. Finely chop the tarragon leaves and stir in. Pour into an ice-cream machine and follow the manufacturer's instructions.

For best results, allow the sorbet to soften slightly before serving by placing in the fridge for 20 minutes beforehand.

¾ cup sugar
5 sprigs of tarragon, leaves picked, stems reserved
2⅔ cups freshly squeezed pink grapefruit juice (about 4–5 grapefruits)

I love inventing cocktails. This is one of my favorites!

PINK GRAPEFRUIT VODKA

Before making the sorbet, scrub the grapefruits, then remove the zest in strips using a potato peeler, cutting away any bitter pith. Empty the vodka into a pitcher, push the grapefruit zest into the now empty bottle, and pour over the vodka; there will be a little left (oh dear).

Leave to infuse in a cool place for up to 2 weeks. Serve drizzled over Pink Grapefruit and Tarragon Sorbet (see above) or use as a base for a cocktail: mix with fresh basil, gomme or another sweet syrup, and pink grapefruit juice; top off with soda and serve over ice.

zest of 4–5 grapefruits
1-liter bottle vodka

#99

Orange and rosemary complement one another beautifully. I've chosen to use blood oranges here, but if they're out of season, don't worry. Try serving with Orange and Rosemary Biscotti (recipe #108) < SERVES 4–6 >

BLOOD ORANGE AND ROSEMARY CRÈME CARAMEL

FOR THE CARAMEL
½ cup superfine sugar
½ cup water

FOR THE CUSTARD
1⅔ cups heavy cream
2 sprigs of rosemary
zest of 2 blood oranges
1 vanilla bean, split
⅔ cup superfine sugar
2 whole eggs
2 egg yolks

1 blood orange, segmented, to serve

Preheat the oven to 350°F.

To make the caramel, put the sugar and water in a small pan and heat over medium heat until melted. Increase the heat and cook until the sugar turns dark amber in color. Pour the caramel into six ramekins and leave to cool.

To make the custard, heat the cream, rosemary, orange zest, and vanilla until simmering. Remove from the heat and leave to infuse for about 30 minutes. Then strain the cream into a pan and heat gently until warm.

Whisk the sugar, eggs, and yolks together. Gently whisk a little cream into the eggs, then whisk in the remaining cream. Skim the surface to remove any air bubbles.

Fill each ramekin with custard and place in a baking pan lined with a kitchen towel (this will keep the ramekins from moving around). Pour enough boiling water into the pan to come two thirds of the way up the sides of the ramekins. Cook for about 1 hour or until the custards are almost set. Remove from the oven and leave to cool in the water. Chill for at least 1 hour, but preferably overnight, before serving.

To serve, dip the bottom of each ramekin in boiling or hot water for a few seconds. Turn the custards out onto plates and garnish with a few blood orange segments.

VARIATIONS

• Vary the citrus and herbs to create your own favorite flavors.

202

monkeys eat the fruit but not the seeds inside

one tree produces 2000 cocoa pods per year – these are the fruit of the tree

the SEEDS = the BEANS

the beans are dried, cleaned, fermented, and roasted – and turned into chocolate

complement with PX sherry – rich, sticky + intense, just like chocolate

a delight for all the senses

add texture with fruity raisins and make a divine chocolate cake

warm, exotic, earthy

serve warm with sour crème fraîche

a spoonful of dreams!

Pedro Ximénez sherry is sweet and intense, packed with rich, toasty fig and raisin undertones. It's like fruit cake in a glass and makes a perfect accompaniment to a gooey chocolate cake. < SERVES 6 >

CINNAMON CHOCOLATE CAKES WITH SHERRY-SOAKED RAISINS AND SHERRY-SPIKED CRÈME FRAÎCHE

Preheat the oven to 350°F. Grease 4-6 dariole molds or tea cups and dust them with cocoa powder.

Whisk all the ingredients for the PX crème fraîche together until smooth and refrigerate for 1 hour before using.

To make the cakes, place the butter and chocolate in a heatproof bowl above a pan of hot water, making sure the bowl doesn't touch the water. Once melted, remove from the heat and leave to cool a little.

Whisk the eggs and sugar together until pale and fluffy, then whisk in the cooled chocolate. Sift the cinnamon, flour, cocoa powder, and salt over the chocolate mixture and fold in.

Spoon the mixture into the prepared molds and place on a baking sheet in the oven for 10–12 minutes only. They should be a little soggy, so a skewer inserted in the center will not come out clean; you should have a lovely fudge-like center instead.

Leave the cakes to cool a little before gently turning out.

To make the PX sherry-soaked raisins, warm the sherry until almost boiling, add the raisins, then turn off the heat and leave to cool. The raisins will become plump and absorb the sherry. Serve at room temperature.

Serve the cakes topped with sherry-soaked raisins and sherry-spiked crème fraîche. If making ahead of time, heat for 10 seconds only in the microwave; any longer and the gooey insides will harden.

FOR THE PX SHERRY-SPIKED CRÈME FRAÎCHE
1 cup crème fraîche
1 tbsp Pedro Ximénez sherry
1½ tbsp light brown sugar

FOR THE CHOCOLATE CAKES
11 tbsp unsalted butter, plus a little more for greasing
5½oz dark bitter chocolate (75 percent cocoa solids)
3 eggs
1 cup superfine sugar
2 tsp ground cinnamon
½ cup all-purpose flour
⅓ cup unsweetened cocoa powder, plus extra for dusting
pinch of sea salt

FOR THE PX SHERRY-SOAKED RAISINS
⅓ cup Pedro Ximénez sherry (available online or in specialty stores)
⅔ cup raisins

VARIATIONS

• Try serving the PX crème fraîche with the Baked Macintosh Apple Cheesecake (recipe #90).

A decadent adult trifle, perfect for a dinner party. Make it in individual glasses or fill up a funky retro trifle bowl. You'll need to start this a day ahead, as the jelly will take about 3 hours to set. < MAKES 6–8 >

PLUM, PORT, AND CHOCOLATE TRIFLES WITH WHITE CHOCOLATE CRÈME FRAÎCHE

BITTER CHOCOLATE AND PORT JELLY

¾ cup superfine sugar

1 cup port

10½oz dark chocolate (70 percent cocoa solids), broken into small pieces

2 sheets gelatin, softened in cold water

FOR THE CREAMY CUSTARD

50g Bird's custard powder

¼ cup superfine sugar

1 cup milk

1 cup heavy cream

1 vanilla bean, split and scraped

15 ladyfingers

½ cup port

FOR THE CARAMELIZED PLUMS

8 plums, halved, pits removed, then cut into thirds

⅓ cup superfine sugar

3 tbsp port

FOR THE WHITE CHOCOLATE CRÈME FRAÎCHE

5½oz white chocolate, broken into small pieces

⅓ cup crème fraîche

½ cup heavy cream

cocoa powder, for dusting

To make the jelly, combine the sugar and port in a saucepan and bring to a boil over medium heat. Add the chocolate and stir until smooth. Remove from the heat, squeeze any excess water from the gelatin, and add to the port and chocolate mixture. Stir to dissolve. Leave to cool a little, then refrigerate until almost set (this will take a few hours) before spooning over the plums.

While your jelly is setting, prepare the custard. Mix the custard powder and sugar with a little of the milk to form a smooth paste. Heat the cream with the remaining milk and vanilla seeds in a saucepan until almost at boiling point. Reduce the heat and slowly add the custard mix, whisking continuously until thickened. Remove from the heat and cover the surface with plastic wrap to prevent a skin from forming. Leave to cool a little while you prepare the ladyfingers and the plums.

Break the ladyfingers into small pieces and divide between individual glasses or place in the bottom of a large bowl. Drizzle with port and top evenly with the slightly cooled custard.

While the custard cools a little more, prepare the plums. Heat a large frying pan and toss the plums with the sugar of your choice. Add the plums to the pan and sear over medium heat for 5 minutes until softened and caramelized. Add a splash of port, then spoon the plums over the custard.

Once the custard and plums are cool, refrigerate until the jelly is almost set. Then spoon the jelly evenly over the plums and refrigerate again until set completely.

Meanwhile, prepare the white chocolate crème fraîche. Place the white chocolate and crème fraîche in a heatproof bowl and place over simmering water, making sure the bowl doesn't touch the water. Stir occasionally, until melted and smooth, then remove from the heat and leave to cool. Whisk the heavy cream until soft peaks form, then fold into the chocolate and crème fraîche. Spoon the jelly over the top and refrigerate for 20 minutes. Serve chilled, dusted with a little cocoa.

208

White chocolate has natural lemon notes. I like to accentuate these by adding some tropical flavors. The good news here is that you don't need an ice-cream machine to make a parfait. < SERVES 4–6 >

WHITE CHOCOLATE PARFAITS

Melt the chocolate in a bowl set over a pan of simmering water and leave to cool.

Whisk the egg yolks until pale.

Place the sugar and 3 tablespoons water in a pan and heat gently until dissolved. Increase the heat until the sugar boils and reaches a temperature of 250°F.

Gradually pour the hot syrup down the side of the bowl while the egg yolks are whisking. Continue to whisk until pale and thick and the mixture leaves a trail for 3 seconds. Whisk in the cooled melted chocolate.

Whisk the cream to form soft peaks then fold into the chocolate mixture with the lime zest and juice, ginger, and lime leaves.

Pour into a terrine mold lined with plastic wrap, stud with the lychees, and place in the freezer.

To serve, turn out of the mold and slice. Serve with passion fruit squeezed over the top or served on the side.

6oz white chocolate

5 egg yolks

½ cup superfine sugar

1⅓ cups heavy whipping cream

zest of 2 limes, finely grated

juice of 1 lime

¾in piece of fresh ginger, peeled and finely grated

2 lime leaves, finely chopped

12 lychees, chopped

2 passion fruits

VARIATIONS

- You could also freeze this parfait in individual molds.

EXTRAS

#103 TAHINI YOGURT SAUCE

1 garlic clove, crushed
1 tsp sea salt
¼ cup tahini
pinch ground cumin
2 tbsp lemon juice
⅔ cup Greek yogurt

Crush the garlic in a mortar and pestle with a little salt to form a paste, transfer to a bowl, and whisk in tahini, 3 tablespoons water, cumin, lemon juice, and yogurt. Refrigerate until required.

#104 WARM CHICKPEA PURÉE

Essentially, this is hummus served warm, but is equally as delicious served cold the next day. You will need to start this recipe the day before.

7oz dried chickpeas
1 tsp baking soda
⅔ cup tahini
3 garlic cloves, crushed
sea salt
juice of 1–2 lemons, to taste
paprika and extra virgin olive oil, to serve

Soak the chickpeas in plenty of cold water overnight.

The next day, drain and rinse the chickpeas, place in a large saucepan, add the baking soda and enough water to cover, and bring to a boil. Simmer gently for about 2 hours, or until very tender, skimming the surface regularly.

Drain the chickpeas, reserving the cooking liquid and a few chickpeas for garnishing. Transfer the chickpeas to a food processor and process to a smooth purée, adding a little of the cooking liquid (about 2 tablespoons for now).

Transfer the purée to a bowl and stir in the tahini, garlic, salt, and lemon juice, to taste. Mix until smooth, adding some of the cooking liquid if the purée is too thick—it should be soft and creamy, but not runny.

Pour into a shallow bowl and spread the purée across it, raising it slightly up the sides. Top with the reserved chickpeas, drizzle with olive oil, sprinkle with a little paprika, and serve.

#105 POMEGRANATE LABNEH

Labneh is strained yogurt that has a firmer cheese-like texture. You'll need to make it the day before you want to serve it.

1½ cups Greek yogurt
2 garlic cloves, crushed
1 tbsp sea salt
1 tsp roasted cumin and coriander seeds, crushed
1 green chile, seeded, finely chopped
pinch sugar
seeds from ½ pomegranate
small bunch cilantro or mint, finely chopped

Mix the yogurt with the garlic and salt. Line a small sieve with a piece of cheesecloth and set over a bowl. Put the yogurt into the cloth and fold over the sides, top with a couple of saucers, and refrigerate. Alternatively, you can tie the cloth and suspend from a shelf in your fridge, but remember to put a bowl underneath! The yogurt will lose excess moisture and will be left with a firmer consistency.

Put the labneh in a bowl. Gently mix with the cumin, cilantro, chile, sugar, and pomegranate seeds.

Sprinkle a plate with the chopped herbs. Shape the labneh into walnut sized balls and roll in the chopped herbs to coat. Refrigerate until required.

212

#106 PICKLED ENOKI MUSHROOMS

Make a batch of enoki mushrooms and store in your refrigerator. Toss through basmati or jasmine rice, or put in a California roll with some avocado. Serve with grilled fish or toss through a Thai chicken or duck noodle salad.

3½oz enoki—golden or white
2 tbsp grapeseed, peanut, or sunflower oil
½ red chile, finely sliced
2 tbsp Shoaxing
1 tbsp superfine sugar
1½ tbsp soy sauce
1½ tbsp rice wine vinegar
2 tbsp sesame oil

Cut the stems off the enoki and separate a little. Heat the oil in a large frying pan and cook the enoki and chile over medium heat until the enoki have softened.

Transfer to a non-metallic bowl and set aside briefly to cool.

Add the remaining ingredients to a small saucepan and warm over low heat until combined. Pour over the mushrooms and leave to infuse for 20 minutes or preferably overnight.

Once cooled, store covered in the refrigerator and serve at room temperature.

VARIATIONS

- Crush some coriander seeds and toss through the enoki while cooking, or sauté some julienne of fresh ginger and add to the mix.
- I like to serve these with rice and red braised mushrooms.

#107 PORCINI SALT

Use this salt to season white fish, scallops, shrimp, or meat.

1oz dried porcini mushrooms
¼ cup coarse sea salt

Grind the porcini in a coffee grinder or blender until powdered. Add the salt and grind until well combined. Store in an airtight container.

VARIATIONS

- This is fabulous tossed through cooked pasta with a little Parmesan.
- Sprinkle onto braised buttered cabbage, new potatoes, corn on the cob, cooked white beans, omelets, or soft-boiled, poached, or fried eggs.

213

#108 ORANGE AND ROSEMARY BISCOTTI

This recipe is kindly donated by Danny Boy—my extremely talented Head Chef and kitchen soul mate! Thank you so much for sharing this with all of us; it complements the Blood Orange and Rosemary Crème Caramel (recipe #99) beautifully. Makes about 40.

1¼ cups all-purpose flour
2 tbsp butter
⅓ cup superfine sugar
½ tsp baking powder
1 sprig of rosemary, finely chopped
zest of 2 oranges
1 egg, beaten

Preheat the oven to 350°F.

Mix the flour and butter together to form a bread crumb consistency. Add the sugar, baking powder, rosemary, and orange zest. Mix to combine. Make a well in the center of the dry mix and add the egg, mixing to form a dough. Roll the dough into a log shape, about 12in long and place on a lined baking sheet. Bake in the oven for 30 minutes. Remove from the oven and leave to cool.

Reduce the oven temperature to 250°F.

Using a sharp bread knife, cut the log into slices of your desired thickness. Place the sliced biscotti back onto the baking sheet and return to the oven to dry out for 30–45 minutes.

#109 DRIED FIG & POLENTA COOKIES

To go with panna cotta (recipe #79).

3oz dried figs, soaked in hot water until softened
7 tbsp unsalted butter, at room temperature
⅓ cup superfine sugar, and extra for baking
2 tsp orange zest, finely grated
2 egg yolks
pinch of sea salt
1¾ cups all-purpose flour
3oz polenta

Preheat the oven to 400°F and line a baking sheet with parchment paper. Drain the figs and cut into small pieces. Cream the butter, sugar, and orange zest until pale and fluffy. Add the yolks one at a time. Sift salt and flour over the creamed butter mix, add the polenta and figs, and beat until combined. Knead lightly for a couple of minutes then roll into a cylinder about 1¼in in diameter, wrap in plastic wrap, and refrigerate for about 30 minutes or until firm.

Unroll the dough onto a sugared or floured surface and cut into cut into ¼in thick slices. Place on a baking sheet, sprinkle with a little sugar, and bake for 10–12 minutes or until lightly golden. Cool on wire racks and sprinkle with a little more sugar. Store in an airtight container until required. You could soak the figs in orange flower water, PX sherry, or port to add an extra flavor hit!

#110 LAVENDER SUGAR

Make a batch of lavender sugar and use for shortbreads, meringues, ice cream, jelly, mojitos, etc!

4 tbsp fresh dry lavender flowers or 2 tbsp dried
¾ cup superfine sugar

Mix the flowers with the sugar or place the lavender and sugar in a food processor to finely chop up the flowers into the sugar. Place in an airtight container. Leave to infuse for a week in a cool dark place to allow the flavors to develop.

#111 FLATBREADS

Flatbreads are quick and easy to prepare. Here's the basic recipe for you to adapt by adding different herbs and spices. You can even add things like finely chopped olives or sundried tomatoes.

¾ tbsp active dried yeast
½ tbsp superfine sugar
¾ cup lukewarm water
3¼ cups all-purpose flour
3 tsp sea salt
1 tbsp olive oil

Combine the yeast, sugar, and water in a bowl and leave in a warm place to ferment for about 10 minutes. Sift the flour into a mixing bowl and add the salt, along with any flavor of your choice, if using. Pour in the yeast mix and olive oil and mix with the end of a wooden spoon to bring the dough together. (If you own a food processor with a dough hook, use this to mix it.)

Turn the dough out onto a lightly floured surface and knead until smooth and elastic. A little oil on your hands will keep the dough from sticking to them. Place the dough in an oiled bowl, cover, and leave in a warm place until it has doubled in size (about 1–1½ hours).

Turn the dough out onto a lightly floured surface and knock it back. Divide into 8 balls, roll out each one to about ¼in thickness, and arrange on a baking sheet lined with parchment paper.

Preheat a grill pan. Brush the flatbreads with a little oil and cook for about 1 minute or until golden on each side.

You can make the dough in advance and keep in the fridge for two days. If you cook the flatbread in advance, warm it through in the oven before serving.

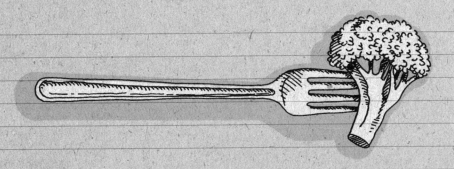

GET CREATIVE

This section is all about YOU!

This is your chance to create and develop your own recipes from mine. Be inspired to experiment with them. The examples on the following pages should get you out of the starting gates. Here are some basic guidelines for you:

* Consider whether the ingredients are in season. If not, adapt with a suitable alternative.
* Take the recipe on a flavor journey. i.e. from a Greek influence to an Asian one.
* Lighten up the recipe. i.e. change lamb to fish. Or do the opposite to add depth.
* Simplify—use only part of the recipe.
* Vary cooking methods—e.g. bbq rather than roast.
* Consider the textures when substituting i.e. change like for like.

217

Be confident! ADAPT - CREATE - TASTE and let the recipes evolve into your own style as you scribble away in the blank pages of this chapter. Make this book your very own.

BIRDS #6

Slow-roasted Paprika Chicken with Butternut Squash, Smashed Butter Beans, and Tomatoes

- replace with boneless leg of lamb as in recipe #19
- try alternative marinade i.e. garlic, dill, lemon as in recipe #19
- use peas instead
- replace with baby potatoes

PORK #14

Porchetta with Rosemary Roasted Potatoes

- try alternative stuffing i.e. chicken liver stuffing from recipe #28
- serve with roasted apples
- replace the pork with a leg of lamb
- accompany with squash as in recipe #6
- try roasting with sage instead of rosemary
- or replace the potatoes with barley

My experiments:

LAMB #21

Braised Lamb Loin with Runner Beans and Tomatoes

marinate the lamb with Moroccan spice paste as in recipe #13

replace or add cooked chickpeas

flavor with honey and orange zest

replace potatoes with sweet potatoes, or omit and serve with couscous

BEEF #22

Veal Chop Topped with Melted Manchego and Quince, with Creamy Sage and Onion Polenta

replace with pork chop

flavor polenta with thyme + Parmesan

replace topping with St. Agur Blue, thyme + apple slices

My experiments:

GAME #31

Pomegranate Marinated Quail, Grilled radicchio, and Bitter Leaf Salad

replace with Middle Eastern chicken marinade (recipe #5)

use lamb instead of quail and serve with the same ingredients

replace with spiced carrot purée + dukkah (recipe #58)

complement with carrot and herb salad (recipe #59)

or serve with eggplant mull, recipe #67

OILY FISH #35

Mackerel with Jalapeño Jelly, Pine Nuts, and Mint

replace with duck breast or leg

exchange with plum and ginger jelly

use this jelly, pine nuts + mint with Veal Chop (recipe #22)

My experiments:

WHITE FISH #38

Pan-fried Sea Bream with

Cauliflower, Pistachio, and Mint Couscous and Cauliflower Purée

- replace with lamb loin
- marinade as in recipe #19 + grill
- serve with cauliflower couscous and purée but...
- replace pistachios with almonds
- and add chopped dates to the couscous

SEAFOOD #42

Baked Clams with Rosemary, White Beans, and Tomatoes

- use raw shrimp instead
- replace with finely chopped ginger, lemongrass, red chile, garlic, and cilantro
- replace with roasted diced squash or pumpkin

My experiments:

225

GRAINS & PULSES #52

Moroccan-Spiced Lentils with

Pan-fried Salmon and Avocado Cream

Go Greek!
Use cinnamon,
lemon, dill, mint,
and garlic, and
add a splash of
red wine vinegar

replace with
grilled leg of lamb
as in recipe #19

serve with
avocado cream

sprinkle with dukkah
- recipe #58

ROOTS #57

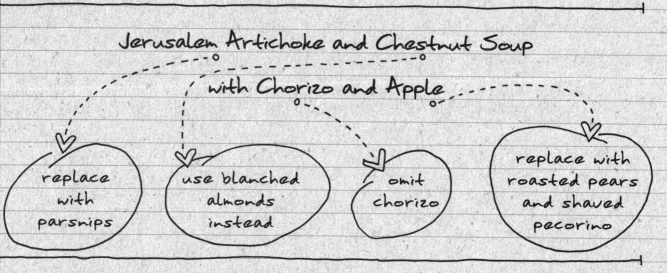

Jerusalem Artichoke and Chestnut Soup

with Chorizo and Apple

replace
with
parsnips

use blanched
almonds
instead

omit
chorizo

replace with
roasted pears
and shaved
pecorino

226

My experiments:

EGGPLANT #64

Eggplant-Wrapped Halloumi with Pomegranate Labneh

replace with feta cheese

flavor with lemon zest + mint

replace pomegranate seeds with dates + almonds (recipe #105)

GREENS #73

Green Olive Gnocchi with Wilted Greens

replace with chopped cooked beets

exchange with beet leaves, chard leaves + baby spinach

top with shaved Parmesan + truffle oil

serve with shredded pheasant (recipe #30)

My experiments:

DAIRY #78

Rhubarb, Rosewater + Ginger Trifle

replace with roasted or fresh peaches

exchange for orange flavored water

replace ginger cake with Madeira cake

BERRIES #84

Raspberry, Amaretti + Greek Yogurt Ice Cream Arctic Roll

replace with bananas

use crumbled honeycomb instead

add or replace with vanilla or chocolate ice cream

roll with cocoa

My experiments:

231

STONE FRUIT #87

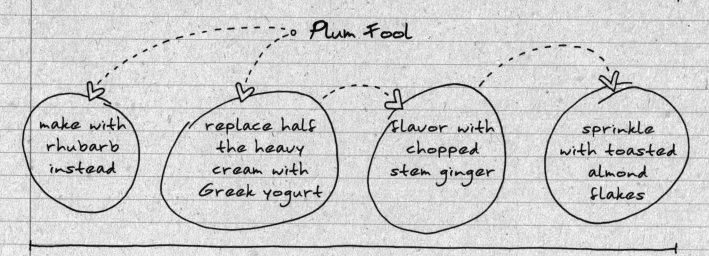

Plum Fool

make with rhubarb instead

replace half the heavy cream with Greek yogurt

flavor with chopped stem ginger

sprinkle with toasted almond flakes

APPLES & PEARS #93

Pear Beignets with Rosemary Sugar and Pear Crème Anglaise

use quince instead

replace with bay leaves

use bay leaf and quince to infuse the poaching liquid instead of pears

My experiments:

CITRUS FRUIT #99

Blood Orange and Rosemary Crème Caramel

replace orange zest with lemon zest

replace with lemon verbena leaves or lemon thyme

serve with lemon and lemon thyme scented biscotti (a version of recipe #108)

CHOCOLATE #100

Cinnamon Chocolate Cakes with

Sherry-soaked Raisins and Sherry-spiked Crème Fraîche

replace with cardamom

replace with chopped apricots soaked in dessert wine

flavor crème fraîche with cardamom seeds

234

My experiments:

INDEX

239

ACKNOWLEDGMENTS

From the bottom of my socks I would like to thank:

Kyle, for the opportunity and her trust in me to write a second book—it's been quite a journey!

To Jenny, my editor, who's listened to my crazy ideas and tried to decipher my writing for the past year! Thanks for your guidance, patience, and for making my dreams a reality and keeping me on the straight and narrow!

To the "A team" who once again worked on my second book:

Jonathan "the one and only photographer" Gregson, who has been an integral part of this book, and whose work I trust and respect. His understanding of my style meant he was able to capture the essence of each dish and bring it to life.

Annie and her assistant, Rachel, who interpreted and prepared the recipes with such stylish results. Mungo—your presence was greatly missed!

Liz Belton, who sourced such beautiful props to complement my recipes perfectly.

To Kath, who's been there every step of the way with her endless support and encouragement; never giving up even through the "tricky stuff," and there certainly have been a few. Your help has been invaluable; you took my vision on board and came up with a truly stunning design that exceeded all my expectations, along with your fabulous illustrations! You have made me feel proud.

To Anne Newman and Nikki Sims, who painstakingly edited the recipes.

Last but not least a few personal thanks to the following:

The one and only "Danny Boy," truly talented chef, for his support and dedication, without which this book would never have happened! Thank you for always holding down the fort—your effort is always appreciated and never goes unnoticed.

To Allison, my best friend, who has always been so generous with her advice and encouragement, I am truly grateful.

To all my friends who have given me the space and time to be totally unsociable while I wrote this book, I've always felt humble knowing you've been there.

To Lucy, Becca, and Kath, for testing some of the recipes!

To all the chefs who've given me the opportunity to succeed and believed in me throughout my career.

xx